According to His Purpose

According to His Purpose

Rev. Terry C. Barber

Belleville, Ontario, Canada

ACCORDING TO HIS PURPOSE
Copyright © 2002, Rev. Terry C. Barber

All Rights Reserved. No part of this publication may be reproduced, stored in a retrieval system or transmitted in any form or by any means – electronic, mechanical, photocopy, recording or any other – except for brief quotations in printed reviews, without the prior permission of the author.

All Scripture quotations, unless otherwise specified, are from the *New King James Version* of the Holy Bible. Copyright © 1979, 1980, 1982. Thomas Nelson Inc., Publishers.

ISBN: 1-55306-370-8

**For more information or
to order additional copies, please contact:**
Rev. Terry C. Barber
8561 E. Shiloh Street
Tucson, Az. 85710
(520) 885-4094

Guardian Books is an imprint of *Essence Publishing,* a Christian Book Publisher dedicated to furthering the work of Christ through the written word. For more information, contact:
44 Moira Street West, Belleville, Ontario, Canada K8P 1S3.
Phone: 1-800-238-6376 Fax: (613) 962-3055
E-mail: info@essencegroup.com
Internet: www.essencegroup.com

Printed in Canada
by
Guardian BOOKS

*I dedicate this book to my loving wife, MaryAnn,
and children, James and Bethany.
When MaryAnn said, "In sickness and in health..."
she really meant it! The pain and suffering
my family has been called upon to endure
over the years is unimaginable.
If not for the grace of God strengthening
and keeping them, surely all would have been lost.*

Table of Contents

1. Amazing Grace 9
2. I Have Learned... 15
3. Seek and Ye Shall Find... 21
4. Born Into the Spirit World 25
5. The Just Live By Faith 33
6. Let Go and Let God 41
7. "You Must Become a Broken Man" 51
8. God is Not a Bubble Gum Machine 63
9. For His Sake 69
10. The True Measurement of Spirituality 73
11. Grow Where You're Planted! 79
12. Ask and Ye Shall Receive 87
13. Go Into All the World and Preach 93
14. Know When to Go 101
15. Whom the Lord Loves He Chastens 109

Epilogue 117
About the Author .119

CHAPTER ONE
Amazing Grace

> *For by grace you have been saved*
> *through faith, and that not of yourselves;*
> *it is the gift of God, not of works,*
> *lest anyone should boast.*
>
> ~Galatians 2:8–9

I was raised in a Methodist Church but never heard the message of the gospel. As a teenager, I struggled with my faults and failures, once asking the pastor of the church how I could overcome lust. He told me that lust was normal and it was all right to lust—even *he* lusted after women.

That first summer after high school, the father of my high school sweetheart hired me to drive port-a-pot and septic tank trucks. The pay was good, and I was able to save a nice chunk of change to help with my college bills for the first year.

During my first year of college, however, my high school sweetheart dumped me for someone else. Devastated, I started experimenting with alcohol and marijuana. The following spring, I came home and resumed working for my former high school sweetheart's father, pumping out port-a-pots and septic tanks.

I was out of control during this period of time—out all night bar-hopping, chasing girls and catching a few. I would come home around 5 a.m. and leave for work an hour later. Even during this very rebellious time in my life, though, God was still watching out for me.

One day, I was driving into Mansfield, Ohio, with two thousand gallons of raw sewage on the back of my truck. Route 13 was a divided highway with single-lane roads intersecting it from time to time. I was traveling at around fifty-five to sixty miles an hour, when a tractor-trailer pulled across my side of the highway from a side road, waiting for traffic to clear on the other side so he could turn left. His trailer completely blocked both lanes on my side of the highway. *No problem*, I thought, *I will just stop and wait for the tractor-trailer to get out of my way*. I put my foot on the brake pedal—and my foot went all the way to the floor! I had no brakes! With the trailer blocking the entire road, there was nowhere for me to go! All I could do was close my eyes and grip the steering wheel, knowing I was about to die in a very horrible traffic accident. The only thing between me and a full load of raw sewage was a window behind me!

As I waited for impact, the truck started bouncing around, from side to side and up and down. Then there was nothing—no bouncing or rattling, nothing but smooth road! I opened my eyes and looked around. I was now on the other side of the tractor-trailer, with nothing but clear road in front of me! In my rearview mirror, I could see that the trailer was still blocking the side of the highway! Immediately, a strange feeling came over me. I was not alone—I knew that God or an angel was with me, even as I lived in my sinful lifestyle.

I dropped out of college in the fall of my second year, before the school could throw me out or I flunked. "Withdraw failing" looked better than a grade of "F." I lived at home with my parents for a while, until I could afford my own apartment, and started working at any job I could find.

Tired of working dead-end jobs and wanting to do something with my life, I enlisted in the Air Force in April of 1977. I wanted to feel like I had a purpose for taking up space in this world. While I was in basic training at Lackland AFB, Texas, I was placed under investigation for my involvement with marijuana before I had enlisted. I was brought before an evaluation board to determine whether I should be discharged. Prior to appearing before the board, I pleaded with God to forgive me. If He would only get me out of this trouble I was in, I promised Him, I would never do any of these bad things again. When I went before the board, I pleaded for mercy and said my use of marijuana was a result of peer pressure. I was granted leniency, and permitted to rejoin my unit and continue with my training.

My promise to God to be good lasted through basic training. In technical school and a few months through my first duty assignment at McCord AFB, Washington State, however, I was drinking heavily again, chasing the skirts from one bar to the next. By the time I was twenty years old, I was a drunk deeply involved in pornography. I could not have a good time unless I was drunk. I was addicted to pornography, always preoccupied with immoral, lustful thoughts and desires. Then one day, I was transferred to a different job, where I would be working with different people. My whole life was about to change.

At work one day, my supervisor and I became involved in a conversation about God. I told him, "I don't believe in heaven, and I pray there ain't no hell." When that little distraction technique did not seem to faze him, I tried another I'd learned sometime during my life of sin. I told him, "I believe God is everywhere—He's in the flowers, the grass, the trees, and even in the air we breathe." None of this seemed to distract my supervisor at all. He just let me talk and then came right back to the subject of Jesus Christ and me. "But of course I'm a Christian!" I argued. "I'm American—aren't we all Christians?"

Then my supervisor asked if he could come over to my place that night to talk about it some more. I said, "Sure, I've got nothing else to do tonight." January 30, 1978, between 7:30 and 7:45 p.m., I gave my life to Jesus Christ. I felt Jesus come into my body and I felt Satan leave. I lost all desire for alcohol. I got rid of all the pornography. The destructive hurt and hate was cleared away from my life. I stopped cursing immediately. My life was filled with the love of God, and for the first time, I felt I had a purpose—I had a reason for being alive! I was not alone anymore. God was with me, and I was at peace with God and myself.

I began sharing Christ with all my friends. They thought I was crazy and wanted nothing to do with me. I went to church as often as the doors were open. When I would come home from church at night, several of my old friends were always sitting on my bed, getting drunk, waiting for me. I would simply crawl in behind them and begin reading my Bible. After a few minutes, it would get quiet. I would look up to find that everyone had left! Before long they found another place to party and my roommate wanted me to move. Jesus began replacing my old friends with friends who loved the Lord and knew Him personally, as I did.

Do not misunderstand—plenty of faults and weaknesses remained in my life. The difference was that now I had someone to whom I could take my problems, instead of going out and getting drunk. Jesus became more than just a historical figure I knew about, and became my friend. God was no longer a judge sitting behind a desk up in the sky somewhere, waiting for me to screw up so He could crack me over the head.

Now I know Him as Jesus reveals Him: as my loving Father who will never leave me or forsake me. God is not waiting for me to screw up so He can do bad things to me—He is waiting for me to look up to Him, with eyes of faith, so He can hold me in His arms. In the years to come, I was about to discover how much God really does want to hold me in His arms.

CHAPTER TWO
I Have Learned...

> *Not that I speak in regard to need,*
> *for I have learned in whatever state I am, to be*
> *content: I know how to be abased, and I know*
> *how to abound. Everywhere and in all things I have learned*
> *both to be full and to be hungry,*
> *both to abound and to suffer need.*
>
> ~Philippians 4:11–12

About a month after I received Christ, I dreamed one night that I was standing behind a large pulpit in a church, preaching the gospel of my Lord Jesus. When I awoke the next day, I had a tremendous burden for the lost and to preach God's Word. In the days that followed, the burden got stronger and stronger.

I called my mother in Ohio to tell her what had happened to me, and that I felt that Jesus was calling me to preach His gospel. My mother responded by telling me that several years ago, while she was praying for me and my brother, the Lord had spoken to her. Both of her sons, He told her, would be saved. One of them would preach the gospel. I accepted that as confirmation that God had called me into the ministry.

In the spring of that year, I received a letter from my mother. Doctors had given my father only months to live, and my mother needed me to come home if I could. As I read the letter, I started to cry. Then I started to worship my Lord Jesus, because I knew the Lord was still on the throne, and He tells us in His Word, "in everything give thanks" (1 Thes. 5:18). My request for a humanitarian reassignment back to Ohio was approved. In May of 1978, I was on my way back home after spending only nine months at my first duty station.

I drove home in a 1975 Toyota pickup truck. It took me eight days to get back to Ohio—the weather was terrible, and my truck was using so much oil that I had to stop every 50 to 100 miles to put another quart of oil in the engine! All my belongings were stashed in the back of the truck, including a small pup tent that did not have a floor. The first day, I stopped in Oregon at a roadside park on top of a mountain. Around 2 a.m., a snowstorm passed through and blew my tent down. I decided that the Lord wanted me to keep traveling, so I just threw everything in the back of the truck and continued down the road.

The next stop was not one I had planned—the snowstorm had left several feet of snow. In Wyoming, the roads were closed and it was going to be several days before they would be open again. So, after I had looked at a map, I headed out with a hitchhiker I had met. I chose a southern route, through the mountains to Denver, Colorado.

The hitchhiker was nice enough, but his use of four-letter words indicated to me that he did not know the Lord. I spent the rest of the day telling this man about the love of my life, the Lord Jesus. The roads were terrible and we came very close on several occasions that day to going over cliffs and losing our lives. Throughout the day, however, I could sense the presence of the Lord—it became quite apparent it was nothing short of a miracle that we made it over the mountains and into Denver. Just outside of Denver, we discovered that the roads were closed there, also. No one was permitted to drive on the road we had just traversed without chains or snow studs—of which we had neither! My hitchhiker friend and I parted company in Denver, and I continued for a while following the snowstorm that was leaving record snowfalls everywhere it went.

Just east of Denver, I was forced to stay in a motel, because it was to cold to sleep in my floorless tent. The next day, I awoke to even *more* snow and nearly impassable roads. I started the day by trying to put another quart of oil in the engine and then sliding out of the parking lot. Praying and asking God for help, I crept along. Then, right in front of me, appeared the answer to my prayers—a large snowplow! I was able to follow the snowplow until I was almost out of the bad weather, when my oil light came on. I had to pull over to the side of the road—what little bit of side there was—to see what the problem was. While car after car tried to squeeze past me, I opened the hood. Oil was everywhere on the inside—apparently, I had forgotten to put the oil cap back on when I put oil in the engine earlier in the day! Here is the miracle: the oil cap was still sitting on top of the radiator where I had left it that morning! I put more oil in the engine, put the oil cap back on, and was on the road again.

Throughout that entire trip, I could sense God's presence there with me in the cab of the pickup truck. I arrived home in Ontario, Ohio, on May 13, 1978.

Since I was still on leave from the military, I didn't have to report to my next duty station at Rickenbacker Air Force Base in Columbus, Ohio, for a couple of weeks. This gave me time to reacquaint myself with my Mom and Dad, as well as reflect on my childhood days there at the house in which I had grown up.

As a child, we didn't have much money. I shared an upstairs bedroom with my brother, and my sister had to walk through our room to get to her room. This didn't provide much privacy for me, but since I didn't know any better, I suppose it really didn't matter.

Since there was no heat duct up to our rooms, in the winter, it was so cold that ice would form on the inside of our windows! My brother and I used to scratch off the ice, making small holes to look out of in order to see what the weather was going to be like that day.

Wasps lived inside the walls—every spring they would come out and we would find them in our beds. I remember, one night, waking up to the hum of a large wasp next to my head *on my pillow*! I often slept elsewhere due to this constant problem.

Even though we were poor, my parents always managed to keep us kids well fed, clothed and sheltered. However, the kids with whom we attended school were, for the most part, far better off then we were. They often let us kids know it, too. I used to hate going to school, and hated coming home even more. I was ashamed of my house and didn't want anyone to know were I lived.

As I thought about these things from the perspective of an adult who had experienced living on his own, the Lord began to show me how tremendous the sacrifices were that my parents endured for my sake. Mom and Dad had truly showed love and commitment to us kids and to each other. Even though we may not have had as much as other kids growing up, our parents loved us and were always there for us. They taught us the importance of family and being together. I realized I was really quite wealthy, after all!

The Lord began to show me that life is much easier to handle when you look at things using His measuring stick rather than the world's. I began to understand a little of what the Apostle Paul was talking about in Philippians 4 when he wrote, *"...I have learned in whatever state I am, to be content...."*

CHAPTER THREE

Seek and Ye Shall Find...

> *But you shall receive power when the Holy Spirit has come upon you; and you shall be witnesses to Me in Jerusalem, and in all Judea and Samaria, and to the end of the earth.*
>
> ~ACTS 1:8

After my arrival home, my mother and my father took me to a Methodist Church they were attending, in the small town of Edison—just outside another small town called Mount Gilead, Ohio. The church was around thirty or forty miles away from my parents' home, but they loved the church and the pastor did not compromise the Word of God, so they did not mind the long drive.

This was a Wednesday night service. When we arrived, late that night, the pastor had already begun his teaching on the book of Acts. As the pastor continued in his presentation, he began to talk about the Baptism of the Holy Spirit. I had been taught that the Baptism of the Holy Spirit was not for today, since I had been born again through a Baptist church; consequently, I stood up in the middle of the meeting and began disagreeing with the pastor, right there in front of the congregation.

After the service, the pastor gave me some teaching tapes on the Baptism of the Holy Spirit. I took the tapes home, and spent the next few days listening to them and reading the Scriptures myself, to find out if what I was hearing on the tapes was true or not. When I had completed my study, it was very apparent that the Baptism of the Holy Spirit was scriptural and that there was nothing in Scripture to support the belief that this experience was not for today. I began praying for the Baptism of the Holy Spirit immediately.

That Sunday, at the church in Edison, I went forward at the altar call to receive prayer for the Baptism of the Holy Spirit. When the pastor laid his hands on me, the Holy Spirit came upon me and knocked me to the floor. I stayed on the floor for several minutes, while under the power of the Holy Spirit. I could sense the presence of God in a greater way then ever before! The experience reminded me of when I was water baptized, back in Tacoma, Washington, at the Baptist church. Coming up out of the water, I felt so clean on the inside—it was as though I was starting all over as a child again. Then I looked up and saw steam coming out of the ceiling and totally covering my body. I could sense God strengthening me and giving me what I needed to face the temptations and testing of my sinful friends back at the dorm where I lived. I was truly taking off the old person I used to be and putting on the new person God wanted me to be in Christ Jesus.

When I picked myself up off the floor of that Methodist church, I still had not had the experience of speaking in tongues—as many of the Scriptures I had read indicated was evidence that I had been Baptized in the Holy Spirit. I wanted the assurance or proof that I had truly experienced the Baptism of the Holy Spirit, so I continued seeking God for this experience, day after day and week after week, for three months. I understood that the Baptism of the Holy Spirit had nothing to do with my earlier salvation experience. The Baptism of the Holy Spirit was to empower me for service and bring me into a more intimate relationship with God. At salvation, the Holy Spirit came inside *me*—at the Baptism of the Holy Spirit, I came inside *the Holy Spirit*. In other words, I was immersed in the Holy Spirit.

One night, two of my friends took me to a United Pentecostal Church camp meeting. At the end of the service, I ran to the altar seeking evidence of my Baptism in the Holy Spirit. It came like a flood of rushing water from the depths of my being. I spoke in tongues for most of the night, still speaking in tongues after getting home and going to bed that night. The presence of God was stronger then ever, and my heart was full of joy and the glory of the Holy Spirit!

My desire to preach the gospel followed me wherever I went. At times, it would be better described as a tremendous burden on my shoulders. The Word of God was like fire in my bones. With no place to release this energy, I was a very frustrated twenty-one-year-old man. My friends and I visited a small Pentecostal church one night that was meeting in the back of someone's home. Worship was powerful and definitely Spirit filled. At one point in the service, the woman who was overseeing the meeting walked up to me and stretched out her hand toward me. She then began speaking to me under the anointing of the Holy Spirit. The Holy Spirit said, "The hand of the Lord is upon you, and

He will take you down a path that you have never thought of before or ever could imagine in your own mind." Those words burned into my spirit, and I knew it truly was God speaking to me. I was so excited, to think that God actually talked to me, that I got up and left before the service was over. I had heard enough in those few words from the Lord to keep me going for months!

CHAPTER FOUR

Born Into the Spirit World

You are of God, little children, and have overcome them, because He who is in you is greater than he who is in the world.

~1 JOHN 4:4

I was sleeping at my mother and father's home in Ontario, Ohio, when the attacks began. Shortly after the Lord spoke to me, the devil began attacking me at night while I slept. In the middle of the night, something invisible to the physical eye would jump on me, and we would begin wrestling on the floor.

While it gripped me, making me unable to speak or move, the evil spirit would talk to me in a language I could not understand. All I could think to do was to plead the blood of Jesus in my mind. When I did this, the tormenting demon would leave. This happened repeatedly for several nights. Then I decided that the room in which I was sleeping was causing the problem, so I anointed the walls and windows with olive oil, and prayed over the room in tongues. The next night, it happened again—but this time when I started to plead the blood of Jesus, the demon started talking in English.

He said, "No, you don't! That's not going to work this time. I've got you this time." I continued anyway, pleading the blood of Jesus in my mind, and the demon left.

I decided to sleep outside in the van on the following night. Everything was fine until just before sunrise. The demon jumped on me again, taking control of my hands, and tried to strangle me. My mouth started growling. Again, I started pleading the blood of Jesus repeatedly in my thoughts until, finally, the demon left. That morning when I got up, the demon spoke to me: "I am inside you now, and you belong to me now." He was a liar, I told him—I had been bought with the blood of Jesus and always would belong to Jesus. I rebuked the demon in Jesus' name and quoted the Scripture in 1 John 4:4, "...He who is in you is greater than he who is in the world."

The next night, I anointed the inside of the van with oil in the name of Jesus, and as I continued in prayer, I felt the van begin to shake and rock from side to side. I opened my eyes and looked up; I saw steam coming through the ceiling and it filled the entire van. This steam pushed me down to the floor of the van, and the Lord Jesus began speaking to me. He said, "I love you with an everlasting love, I am with you and I have called you to Myself." He said, "You will never be attacked in this way by the devil again. I will protect you and keep the devil from you from now on." I went to sleep in the midst of sweet peace. The devil has never again attacked or tormented me in that way.

Shortly after this experience, I had another close encounter with the spirit world. One night at my duty station, Rickenbacker Air Force Base in Columbus, Ohio, my friends and I decided to go downtown. We planned to do some street witnessing and maybe some preaching on the street corners of the Ohio State University.

As we prepared to leave the base, a man dressed in civilian clothes stopped us in the parking lot. We had never seen the man before and never saw him again after that. Now, looking back on the incident, I wonder if the man may have been an angel. He came to us with a strange request—he asked us if we could go over to the commissary on base and help take apart some shelves that the base was donating to the Salvation Army. All three of us felt a tug on our heart strings to say yes, but we had already made plans for the evening and didn't want to change them, so we continued on our way down town to the Ohio State campus.

My friend had turned the car radio on just outside the gates of the base. We listened as Catharine Coleman began speaking, it seemed, right to us. She started preaching from the Gospel of Matthew, where Jesus taught about how

> *...I was hungry and you gave Me no food; I was thirsty and you gave Me no drink; I was a stranger and you did not take Me in, naked and you did not clothe Me, sick and in prison and you did not visit Me.' Then they also will answer Him, saying, 'Lord, when did we see You hungry or thirsty or a stranger or naked or sick or in prison, and did not minister to You?' Then He will answer them, saying, 'Assuredly, I say to you, inasmuch as you did not do it to one of the least of these, you did not do it to Me.' And these will go away into everlasting punishment, but the righteous into eternal life* (Matt. 25:42–46).

Every word Sister Catherine spoke seemed to strike us right in the center of our hearts. We looked at each other and at the same time said, "Let's go back and help take apart the shelves at the commissary!"

We made a U-turn and drove back to the base. When we arrived at the commissary and went inside, we could not find the man who had asked us to come and do the work, so we just joined in with everyone else. One of my friends, who was very zealous for the Lord, had the habit of getting me involved with all his schemes, consequently getting me into trouble. He had noticed that two of the other workers were deaf and mute.

My friend brought these men to my attention and said, "We are Pentecostal Christians. We believe the Bible is the Word of God and that Jesus still heals people. We should go over there and lay hands on those guys and heal them!" I was rather reluctant to get involved, but my friend persisted. He began shaming me, accusing me of not believing the Bible. So, in order to save face, I agreed to go with him to pray for these men.

We wrote "We are Christians, we believe the Bible teaches you can be healed. Would you like us to pray for you?" on a piece of paper. One of the men got very excited when he read our note. He wrote back, on the same paper, that he was a Christian, too, and would love to have us pray for him. The other man just shook his head and walked off. We then showed our fellow Christian a passage of Scripture, Mark 16:17,18, that says, *"These signs shall follow them who believe: ...they will lay hands on the sick and they will recover."* The man, who seemed to be in his mid forties, became even more excited when he read this verse. Nodding his head, he started jumping up and down. As we walked out of the building and around the corner, where we could pray for him in a more private place, the Holy Spirit came upon me so powerfully that I felt I would explode in joy. As this happened, a tremendous sense of faith seemed to fill my entire being. There was no question in my mind—this man was going to be healed. God was going to perform a miracle here! Later, my friend, who had gotten me into this in the first place, told me he was fighting all kinds of doubt and was very afraid it was not going to work.

When we turned the corner of the building, I looked around, and to my wonderment, saw that some of the other people in the building were filing out to see what we were going to do. Quickly and confidently, I placed my hands on the ears of the man and began praying aloud, "In the name of Jesus Christ of Nazareth, I bind the deaf spirits in this man's ears and command them to come out!" Then I prayed for God to completely heal these ears and let this man hear. When I clapped my hands loudly next to his ears, the man nearly jumped out of his skin with joy, nodding his head that he could hear! Then I placed my hands on his mouth and began praying in like fashion as before (remember, that man had never, in his entire life, spoken a word or heard a word— he was going to require some teaching). When I was done, I spoke into each ear the word "baby." The man repeated back to me, "Baa-bee." Everyone, even the curious spectators, started jumping up and down for joy and praising God!

We ran back into the building, telling everyone we saw that Jesus had healed this man. "He can hear and talk!" The whole place was jumping with excitement when we were approached by the lady who was supervising the two deaf and mute men and had been signing to them to tell them what to do. She said, "This man can't talk—he has never heard or spoken a word in his entire life!"

I said, "Watch this!" I then spoke the word, "baby" into his ear again, and the man replied, "baa-bee". The woman fainted right there on the spot! We started having church and ran out of the building, praising Jesus.

The Lord began using us often in those days. We witnessed in our workplace to our co-workers and supervisors. We would go downtown and do street witnessing, or sit on park benches and witness to people as they walked by. Jesus told His disciples, *"to be wise as serpents and harmless as doves"* (Matt. 10:6), so we devised plans of attack on poor, unsuspecting sinners! When we came across someone sitting alone on a park bench, one of us would approach first and just sit down next to that person—not saying anything, just sitting there. Then a few minutes later, another of us would walk up and sit on the opposite side of the unsuspecting stranger. Then we would pretend we did not know each other and strike up a conversation with each other about Jesus with the stranger still sitting between us! It was great and a lot of fun. Before long, the stranger would either join in or run away.

One night, my friend and I went to one of the local malls in Columbus, Ohio. We had several hundred gospel tracts with us and we started passing them out to everyone we saw. After a couple hours, we had distributed almost all of our tracts when my friend saw a sign on a vendor's cash register that said, "We accept Master Card" and, of course, it had a little picture of the Master Card logo. Well, it just so happens that my friend had a card that looked just like the Master Card logo—only it said, "Give Christ charge of your life." My friend stuck this tract over the vendor's sign. It was a perfect fit, but when the vendor saw what he'd done, he called the police. He then ripped the tract off his sign and grabbed us, to hold us until the police arrived. The police took down our names and the name of the units we belonged to out at the base before escorting us off the premises with a stern warning. They promised to call our First Sergeants in the morning.

The next day came and passed for me with no phone call or trouble from my First Sergeant. My friend, however, was ordered to report to his First Sergeant's office immediately. Being ordered to go to your First Sergeant's office was not on the list of favorite things to do. If you have done well, the First Sergeant is a wonderful person to see. However, the First Sergeant knows just how to make your life miserable when wrongdoing is suspected!

My friend entered the office shaking in his shoes. He knew the First Sergeant was an unbeliever—they had had confrontations over religion before, so he was sure he was in big trouble. However, the First Sergeant was not at his desk. Someone else was sitting there. He was filling in for the First Sergeant, who was away for the day. The replacement was a born-again Christian! He offered congratulations and encouragement to keep up the good work and they worshiped God together there in the office—praise God!

CHAPTER FIVE
The Just Live By Faith

*And let us not grow weary
while doing good,
for in due season we shall reap
if we do not lose heart.*

~GALATIANS 6:9

In September of 1978, I decided it was time to seriously pursue my calling to the ministry. For this reason, I requested an early release from active duty to the Air National Guard. Due to the low demand for people in my career field, and my father's poor health, and, of course, God's control, my request was granted!

I was a civilian again by October and living at home with my parents for the time being. One of my friends also got out early. We planned to open a Christian coffee house in Mount Gilead, Ohio, since by this time I had become very close to the pastor of the Methodist church there (the same one with whom I had argued over the Baptism of the Holy Spirit). My friend and I were going to rent an old dry cleaning storefront on Main Street and some of the people in the church were helping us get started. Before things could ever get off the ground, though, my friend backed out and moved to Pennsylvania.

In January 1979, I found a job in a box factory working from eleven at night until seven in the morning. The box factory was just outside Edison and Mt. Gilead. Since I was still living with my parents in Ontario, my drive one way to work took about an hour. Northern Ohio in the winter was not always such a great place to drive, with snowstorms blowing through from time to time—usually when it was time for me to drive to or from work.

One night, as I drove home from a church service in one of these snowstorms, I tried to traverse a steep hill in near-zero visibility. About halfway up the hill, my truck started slowly sliding over into the opposite side of the road. At that moment, there was no oncoming traffic—at least, as far as I could tell. I tried desperately to get my truck back over on the right side of the road, but it wasn't working. Then things got a lot worse: not only was I on the wrong side of the road, the truck stopped moving! Now I was just sitting there, on the wrong side of the road, with my tires spinning.

Just as I thought things couldn't get any worse, things got worse! Headlights of an oncoming car peaked out at the crest of the hill and were shining in my eyes. Needless to say, I started praying, "Oh God, please get me out of this and I'll never do anything bad again." I was praying just the way I used to before I became a real born-again Christian.

However, I stopped right in the middle of my prayer—I wasn't *doing* anything bad that I needed to stop or repent of. I had a clear conscience before God. I didn't need to make any "deals" with God anymore—He was my loving Father to whom I could go anytime I wanted. Just as I had this realization, my truck slowly slid back over on the right side of the road. I drove straight up the hill and home like someone was pushing from behind. Was it a miracle? It sure felt like one, and it's a great feeling to know when trouble comes, I don't have to go through some kind of repentance ritual to get out of it.

Several occasions on the road that winter seem now to have been visits from, perhaps, an angel. One clear, sunny morning (highly unusual during an Ohio winter), after getting out of work, I was driving home. As I came over a small hill, right in front of me a large snowdrift stretched across the road. I couldn't stop in time and slammed right into it! I lost control of the truck and, of course, out in the middle of nowhere was a telephone pole which I hit head-on. I struck my head on the steering wheel and really 'rung my bell'! My knee was also injured—as I crawled out of the truck, it was hurting really badly and bleeding.

As I said, I was out in the middle of nowhere. It may not have been the end of the world, but it sure seemed visible from there! I started crying out to God for help—there wasn't a house anywhere, or a car, nothing. I didn't know what to do, so I started slowly walking back the way I came, praying and crying as I went. Then, all of a sudden, I heard a noise behind me. Appearing out of nowhere was a car with a man and woman sitting in the front seat. They asked me if I would like a ride back to town! I do not know where they came from, or how they just appeared like that, but of course I said "yes," and they drove me to my pastor's house. After they dropped me off, they drove away and I never saw them again. Was it a miracle? It certainly felt like one!

Shortly after that, I found an apartment large enough to start "The Cornerstone," my envisioned street ministry. It was slow going at first—in fact, many nights passed when I was the only one *at* "The Cornerstone."

My father died in February, of cancer, and I have always been grateful to God that He gave me the opportunity to minister to my Dad before he died and to know that one day I would see my father again in heaven.

At the box factory, the work was hard but had plenty of variety, at least at first. I started out as a warehouse man, but then I transferred to a feeder position. For eight hours a night, I stood in front of this machine, about 35 feet long. My job was to feed stacks of pre-cut cardboard sheets into the front of this machine that would fold and glue the sheets into various boxes. At the other end of the machine, someone else gathered the boxes and placed them in larger boxes for shipping. In the middle, between us, a maintenance man made sure the machine continued working right. The machines often jammed, so we really had to watch them closely. The moment I saw the machine start to jam, I was supposed to push a big red button in front of me. The sooner we stopped the machine the better, because this kept the jam from worsening and made it easier to fix.

The maintenance man that worked on my line had a very small vocabulary. Most of the words he knew contained only four letters. He also used my Lord's name in vain a lot. One night, I told him he was going to go to hell if he didn't repent of his sin. He did not appreciate my opinion on the matter and became very angry. Needless to say, our relationship went downhill from there. He started using curse words whenever he saw me, as a way to torment me.

The Just Live By Faith

The box factory was a very noisy place and unless everyone was on break, it was difficult to hear much, short of shouting at one another. So, most of the time, I was off in my own little world, just singing and praising God in "tongues," because no one could hear what I was saying anyway.

One night, my machine started seriously jamming up. I was really praising God and not paying much attention to it. Off in the "Spirit," I hadn't noticed the problem until it was very, very bad and the maintenance man jumped up screaming at me to shut off the machine. It was too late—the damage was already done.

The maintenance man came running at me, yelling and cursing, using my Lord's name in vain. By then, the break bell had rung, so everyone in the factory stopped working and watched us. I asked the man what his mother's name was. He asked me why I wanted to know that. I told him, "The next time the machine breaks down, I am going to use your mother's name in vain so you'll know how I feel when you use my Heavenly Father's name in vain." The maintenance man did not like my idea. He chased me through the warehouse, yelling and cursing along the way, while everyone else was watching.

As I was running, I decided to ask the Lord what I should do. Fortunately, the Lord was right there and gave me an idea. I stopped running and turned around. Looking at the man coming at me, I pointed my finger at him and I said, "I rebuke you, in the name of Jesus!" Nothing happened at first—the man was still coming at me. So I said it again: "I rebuke you, in the name of Jesus!" Suddenly, the man stopped right in his tracks. He started shaking and stuttering. The look on his face was one of terror. He couldn't say anything, as though someone had hold of his tongue. Then he turned around and started running in the other direction, away from me!

Since everyone in the factory saw and heard what had happened, it wasn't long before I was summoned to see the boss in his office. I received a lecture about how the work area was not the place for religion. My boss told me that if I talked about Jesus any more, I could lose my job. I had to obey God, not men, I told him—and since God had told me to talk about Jesus as much as I could, I intended to continue talking about Jesus in the work area. Then the Lord gave me an idea. I told my boss, "I will make a compromise with you. I will not talk about Jesus unless someone asks me a question about Jesus." The boss was excited about that idea and agreed with this compromise.

When we had finished talking, I opened the door to go back out to work and all these people were standing outside gathered in a large crowd around the door. Everyone was asking me questions about Jesus! One after another, people came to me wanting to know more about my Lord. One woman asked me, "What does 'rebuke' mean?"

That was the beginning of a great ministry opportunity there in the box factory. I still was threatened from time to time by the maintenance man, but continued to stand my ground with him—he left me alone for the most part. The boss moved me back over to the warehouse job, which was the job I preferred, anyway.

Many people heard the gospel in the box factory. Some even came to my apartment to talk about the Lord in more detail. No one gave their heart to Jesus, though, no matter how hard I tried to get them to see the truth. I must have talked in detail to twenty or thirty people with no one praying to receive Christ.

In the spring of 1979, I felt the need to better prepare myself to answer God's call on my life to preach the gospel. The Cornerstone street ministry had not exactly flourished the way I had originally envisioned. However, it did show me that I had a lot to learn about the Bible and being in the ministry in general. Around this same time, I received a magazine in the mail from R.W. Shambach's Evangelistic Ministries. I don't know how I got on their mailing list—at the time, I had never even heard of R.W. Shambach before. In fact, that was the only correspondence I ever received. However, in the magazine, an article about East Texas Bible College, in Tyler, Texas, prompted me to write a request for information about the school.

The school responded, and in just a few weeks I was accepted and scheduled to start in the fall of 1979. There was one small problem: school would start in two months and I did not have enough money. I prayed and asked God if He wanted me to go to this school. Would He confirm this by providing the money for the first year? I needed $2,000. The day I left for Bible college, I had $2,001.

A few weeks prior to my departure, in the attic of the factory, the Lord gave me the privilege of leading a young man, only eighteen years of age, to Christ. Oh, the joy that night brought to my heart! This was the first person I had ever led to Christ. In the weeks to follow, I had the difficult task of trying to disciple him. I was not very successful—when I left Mount Gilead in August 1979 to attend Bible college, he was still struggling with bad language and chewing tobacco.

I had felt like I had failed in my first assignment and was discouraged for some time about it. When I had been in Bible college for one year, however, I received a letter from this new convert of mine, in which he told me that after I had left, he'd visited a small Pentecostal church in Mount Gilead. There he was baptized in the Holy Spirit and found a new zeal for the things of God. He then took his new-found faith into the workplace—the box factory—and revival broke out in the factory! Many of the people to whom I had spent hours talking about the Lord were led to Christ by this young man!

CHAPTER SIX
Let Go and Let God

"...Not by might nor by power, but by My Spirit,"
Says the LORD *of hosts.*

~ZECHARIAH 4:6

Two weeks before I was to leave for Bible college, I prayed with my mother about finding a wife. I told my Mom I was giving up on ever finding a wife and no longer intended to pursue the matter. I was going to be celibate for the rest of my life. I was going to devote my entire life to doing nothing but serving my Lord. That was all God was waiting to hear from me. As soon as I gave up, I released Him to do His work.

I met MaryAnn in Dallas, Texas, where we were stationed at an Air National Guard base. We were both full-time students in separate Bible colleges—I was going to East Texas Bible College in Tyler, Texas, and MaryAnn was a student at Christ for the Nations in Dallas. The first time I saw MaryAnn was at my first weekend guard drill after moving to Texas to go to Bible college.

I remember the troops were having a beer blast around the campfire while I managed to find a couple of Christians to have a prayer meeting with during an overnight bivouac in an old cow pasture in the middle of nowhere. MaryAnn, wearing fatigue pants and a white tee-shirt, came waltzing up to our little meeting with a guy on each arm (later I found out the guys were just for protection).

The moment I saw her, I sensed a strong burden for her in my spirit. I wondered if she was a Christian and began praying for her salvation. The two guys with her didn't have a clue about spiritual matters and it made for a very different night. It was the first time I ever saw anyone singing "Amazing Grace" with a beer in one hand and a cigarette in the other.

The next morning there was a church service on one of the buses, and MaryAnn showed up. Again, the moment I laid eyes on her, my stomach turned flip-flops and I began having this tremendous burden for her. I didn't know what to do, so I just prayed for her.

I didn't see MaryAnn for an entire year afterward, even though the guard base to which we were assigned had only around 100 people on it. During the annual two-week summer training session, I was walking down the hall of one of the maintenance buildings checking on one of the bench stock supply rooms. There she was, right in front of me! I still didn't even know her name but as soon as our eyes met, those same feelings returned. She said, "hi," and I said, "hi" back to her, and then I left the building to begin praying for her.

I prayed that if God wanted me to witness to her, then let me see her again and provide an opportunity for me to talk to her. As I rounded the corner of the building, I no sooner got the words out of my mouth and there she was again, right in front of me. We talked for a few minutes, just small talk—mostly about the weather, since it was over 100 degrees outside that day. Then, as we were going our separate ways, she said, "Think about me while you're in your air-conditioned office and I'm out here in this heat!" I said, "Sure will." Under my breath, I said to myself, "I will also pray for your salvation."

Later that day, as I prayed for her in one of the warehouses, the power and presence of God was all over me. God said, very clearly to my inner man, "She is to be your wife!" I was almost knocked to the floor. I said to the Lord, "But God, I don't even know her name!" Immediately, my heart was flooded with feelings of love for her like I had never felt for anyone ever before in my entire life! Obviously, I did not get much sleep that night. I kept tossing and turning; I could not get her out of my mind. I still didn't know her name and didn't even know if she was a Christian.

The next day, my supervisor told me to go over to the infirmary to be immunized—the military is big on immunization. I went over to do my duty and get my shots. The line was long. I knew I was going to be there a long time. I turned around, and lo and behold, there she was *again*, standing right behind me! By then I was certain this was no coincidence—this was God's handiwork. I had been at this air station every month for an entire year and never seen her here other than that first time at the overnight bivouac!

As we talked, I finally learned her name and that she had moved to Dallas from a place back east called Brentwood, New York. I wanted very badly to find out if she was a Christian, so after I got my shots, I came back out to her and said, "Praise the Lord! I only had to get five shots!" I said this hoping to get a response from her that would give me some kind of clue as to where she was spiritually. However, it didn't work—all she did was smile. I *still* didn't know if she was a Christian.

Another sleepless night passed. The next morning, as I walked in from the parking lot, there she was again! We started talking and I asked MaryAnn how her ear was doing (she'd told me the day before, while we were standing in line for our shots, that an ear infection was bothering her a lot). A big grin came over her face and she said, "Praise the Lord! I went to a prayer meeting last night and had my friends pray for me. Now my ear is feeling much better. The Lord healed me!" That's right, MaryAnn was a Christian also. We started having church right there in the parking lot!

That night after work, I went over to MaryAnn's place to visit. She sat on one side of the room and I sat on the other side. We sat and talked about our lives and how we each met the Lord and everything in between. We talked for around four hours that first night—that was all we did—and then I went home. No kiss, just goodbye. (MaryAnn thought that was the strangest date she had ever been on with a guy.)

The next night, we went on our second date. MaryAnn was going to show me Dallas. All night long, I wanted desperately to put my arm around her, but felt like that would be wrong. I didn't want to give her the wrong impression. We returned to her place and sat on the couch for a few minutes talking, when the magic moment hit us. Looking into each other's eyes, we kissed! It was like "Love, American Style"—an old television show about American romance. Fireworks went off all over the place. My heart must have skipped at least two beats! I told MaryAnn that God had spoken to me and told me she was to be my wife. MaryAnn responded, "Unless God speaks to *me* about it, I'm not marrying anyone. I just want to be friends and go slow for now."

MaryAnn's response was devastating! I was convinced that God had spoken to me, and I was having all these feelings about her—it *had* to be God. As time went on, I decided maybe it wasn't God. Maybe it was just my flesh. I stopped seeing MaryAnn. Whenever she came to my office looking for me, I hid in the warehouse.

I managed to keep my distance this way for about three months. During this time, I started writing letters back and forth with another woman who had graduated the year before me. We arranged to meet over Thanksgiving break, in Ohio, so I could introduce her to my mother. Well, I'd already told Mom about MaryAnn and the whole story of how we met. When I introduced my mom to this other girl, the first words out of Mom's mouth were, "Where is MaryAnn? This is not MaryAnn! MaryAnn is the girl you're to marry—not this girl!" Needless to say, *that* was the worst Thanksgiving I had ever had.

When I returned to Bible college, I called the girl—who lived in Wisconsin—and broke off the relationship. Somehow, I had got it in my head that it was my lot in life to suffer for Jesus and this relationship was part of that suffering—I was to marry this woman even though I knew I wouldn't be happy.

Then, in prayer, the light came on! I realized that God did not work that way. God works from the inside out, not the outside in! The devil works from the outside in, through outward circumstances designed to make us miserable. But our loving Father God works from the inside out, causing us to completely enjoy whatever the will of God for our lives may be. God works on our insides to prepare us for the task ahead, so that even though to others the task may seem horrible, to us, it is the most wonderful opportunity in the world.

After this realization, I knew I was right about MaryAnn. Truly, it *was* the will of God for us to be married! With this conviction on my heart, I made the long drive from Tyler to Dallas for guard drill. As I entered the guard base, right there at the front door was MaryAnn, waiting for me. I could not hide from her this time. MaryAnn said she wanted to talk to me that night after work, so I agreed to meet her and go for a walk at a park to talk.

That night she told me that God had been dealing with her and showing her that I was right about us getting married. She also said she wanted to go slow and just be friends for a while before moving into a more serious relationship. I heard the part about me being right about marriage—that was it! I was on cloud nine. We walked and talked there, in the park, for hours that seemed like minutes. There were some tennis courts there in the park, so we started playing a game of tennis without a ball or tennis rackets. It was crazy and fun! This guard drill was held the first weekend of December, so it would not interfere with Christmas.

When I got back to Tyler, I wasted no time in calling my Mom to tell her the news. I then made plans to get MaryAnn a "friendship ring" for Christmas, and told my Mom all about it. I decided, since she wanted to start out slow and just be good friends at first, that the most appropriate thing to do would be to get her a "friendship ring."

I spent Christmas break in Dallas with some friends to

whom MaryAnn had introduced me. On Christmas Day, MaryAnn and I went for a walk. It was strange seeing people watering their lawns on Christmas Day, since we were both from back east—MaryAnn from Long Island, New York, and me from Mansfield, Ohio. When we came back to the house, I gave my Christmas present to MaryAnn. She opened the present and exclaimed, "An engagement ring! We're engaged!" I said, "What, ah... Yeah, right! An engagement ring—that's right, we're engaged!"

I did not want to tell her I had actually intended it to be a friendship ring, so I just kept my mouth shut about that small detail. Later, I called my mom and told her the news. Mom was cautious—"What, are you *sure* she thinks it's an engagement ring? She really thinks you're engaged?" I said, "Yeah, she really does!" MaryAnn overheard the conversation, and I had to explain what had happened. Then I got down on one knee and made it official.

Our engagement lasted about one year; during this time, the Lord had a lot of work to do to prepare us for our life together as husband and wife. MaryAnn personally met my mother for the first time a few months after our engagement. Mom was in a gospel choir that traveled around the U.S. singing in various churches. We arranged to meet up with her and her group in a small town in southern Texas called Columbus.

Members of the church in which my mother's choir was singing billeted people in their homes. Not knowing my mom and MaryAnn had never met, the church member put them in the same house together—in the same room, sleeping in the same bed! Needless to say, MaryAnn was a nervous wreck the entire weekend! It all worked out fine, though. My mom loved MaryAnn and gave us her engagement ring that my Dad had given to her, and suggested we not wait to get married—just go to the local court house and get married. We could not do that. MaryAnn's parents had not even met me yet, and MaryAnn wanted me to go out to Brentwood to ask her father for her hand in marriage. Yes, that's right—it was now going to be *my* turn to be nervous!

I'd made the mistake of writing MaryAnn's mother a letter in which I told her I was going to be the priest of the family. Right away, she thought I was going to try to make MaryAnn my slave or something, and knew MaryAnn would not stand for that. So, with that little misunderstanding still brewing, we arrived in New York. It took about a week before MaryAnn's mom found me to be acceptable, and for me to conjure up enough courage to ask her father for MaryAnn's hand in marriage. When I finally did, her dad's response was, "There she is—go for it!"

My last year of Bible college had its share of challenges, but probably the most difficult was dealing with the school's policy on relationships with the opposite sex. No one, according to school policy, was to be engaged or have a romantic relationship of any kind with another student while school was in session.

After careful consideration, I decided I was not in violation of this rule for two reasons. One, we got engaged during winter/Christmas break, so school wasn't in session. Two, MaryAnn was not a student at that school, so I wasn't having a romantic relationship with another student.

However, the school board was not as excited and happy for us as we were when they learned of my engagement to MaryAnn. I was asked to appear before the board for a formal hearing. After I pointed out the loopholes in their rules, they dismissed me from the hearing and said they would notify me of their decision.

The board never got back to me with their official decision! Unofficially, though, they made very clear to me that they wanted me to break off our engagement and take back the engagement ring.

When I told MaryAnn how the school felt about our engagement, she said she would never break off our engagement for them or give back my ring. She said, "I'm not a student at your school, and they have no authority over me!" Needless to say, my relationship with my school was slightly strained after this, and even though I continued to maintain excellent grades in all my classes, I was not considered a candidate for valedictorian at my graduation because of my engagement to MaryAnn. Oh well, it was worth it!

CHAPTER SEVEN
"You Must Become a Broken Man"

> *"...My grace is sufficient for you, for My strength is made perfect in weakness."*
>
> ~2 Corinthians 12:9

In the spring of 1981, I was preparing to graduate from Bible College. I felt I was ready to turn the world upside down for the gospel. I was young, only 23, and in good health. I loved Jesus and was ready to give my life for His sake, or so I thought. One morning, the Lord spoke to me while I was in prayer. As clearly as if I was carrying on a conversation with a friend, He said, "You must become a broken man before I can ever use you." Little did I know exactly what was involved in this "breaking."

As I looked for ministry opportunities after graduation, I began getting bloody noses from walking into closed doors. Nothing seemed to be open for me in any of the ministry fields in which I was interested, but this would soon be the least of my challenges.

At that time, I was working for a furniture company, driving a truckload of furniture from Dallas to Houston to Austin and back to Dallas. The trip would usually take two or three days. On one of the trips, I hadn't gotten enough sleep the night before because of some noisy downstairs neighbors playing their stereo too loud all night.

About halfway to Houston, I fell asleep behind the wheel. When I woke up, I was knocking down reflector stakes on the side of the road! Startled, I immediately reacted by turning my front wheels back up towards the highway. The truck turned over, at least one complete rotation, and came to a stop right-side-up again. The top of the truck had ripped open and all the furniture that had been inside was now scattered all over the highway.

There were no seat belts in the truck, so I went flying all over the inside of the cab. When the police and an ambulance arrived, in order to get me out, they had to pry the door open. I was placed on a stretcher and put in the ambulance. One of the rescue workers, trying to keep me from going into shock, kept telling me to say something. She kept saying repeatedly, "Say something, say something!" So, I looked up at her and shouted, "Praise Jesus!" She replied, "Be quiet—don't say anything. Stop talking!"

Suffering from whiplash and dizzy spells, I was not able to get around very well for several months after the accident. At this same time, MaryAnn had come down with a severe case of strep throat, so she also needed nursing. Fortunately, Randy, my brother, had recently moved down to Dallas from Ohio. Randy was a blessing from the Lord—he nursed us both back to health, and the Lord used the situation to bring Randy and me back together.

We have been very close ever since. As the Scripture teaches,

> *And we know that all things work together for good to those who love God, to those who are the called according to His purpose* (Romans 8:28).

MaryAnn and I were married January 23, 1982. A few weeks before our wedding, as I was putting on my uniform and preparing to go to an Air National Guard weekend drill, I had this tremendous desire to re-enlist into active duty with the Air Force again. I loved my uniform and I loved wearing it! I began praying about the idea, and as I was praying, the Lord began speaking to me. He wanted me to re-enlist, He told me, so that through the military, He would send MaryAnn and me to places around the world where countries were closed to the gospel. I told the Lord I would go anywhere in the world He wanted me to go! But what about MaryAnn—how did she fit into the equation? Would she agree to go with me?

When MaryAnn came by to get me for the guard drill, I told her about the experience and asked her how she felt about my re-enlisting. She said she didn't mind at all and actually thought it was a good idea. When I mentioned it would mean going to foreign countries, MaryAnn said she would follow me wherever the Lord led us. I enlisted in the active duty Air Force on January 15.

After our wedding, we left for our honeymoon. I was so excited that I forgot to pack clothes. I didn't realize this until we arrived at our destination, so after we checked into the hotel we had to go shopping for clothes! After our honeymoon we continued on our journey to our first duty station, Scott Air Force Base, Illinois. We were there for three years.

Assigned to the Clothing Sales section in base supply, it didn't take me long to notice my supervisor was a very ungodly man who had no interest in the things of God and used four-letter words on a continual basis. I began praying for an opportunity to share my faith in Christ with him. After several months I noticed my supervisor wasn't going home after work at night—he was sleeping in the office and looked very distraught and unkempt. One morning he called me into his office and closed the door behind me. He knew I was a preacher, he told me. He began telling me his problems and crying like a baby. Between sobs, he told me that a woman had called his wife and told her he was sleeping with one of the female airmen in the base trailer park. This was not true, but his wife did not believe him and a couple of nights before she had come at him with a pair of scissors, intent on killing him! He loved his wife, he told me, and only wanted them to get back together again.

I shared Christ with him and we prayed together for him and his wife. The anointing of the Holy Spirit came upon me and I prayed, "Lord, I pray that You would send Your Holy Spirit upon the woman who has been spreading these lies and convict her of her sin. Holy Spirit, cause her to repent and call my supervisor's wife and tell her the truth. Heal their marriage and all for Your glory, in Jesus' name!"

The next day, my supervisor came into the office with a big grin on his face and was all cleaned up and well groomed. He told me that last night the woman who had been spreading the lies called his wife and asked for forgiveness. She was crying and told his wife she had made it all up and was very sorry. She told her she didn't know why, but that something had come over her, making her feel very bad about what she had done and she was miserable. She knew she had to call and make things right! Praise God!

I had been looking for the opportunity to be used by God ever since we had arrived at Scott AFB. I wanted to preach and minister to adults—of course, God's plan was different. We became heavily involved in a local church working with children. I had little to no interest in ministry to children, but MaryAnn had a burden for them and began helping out with children's church while I sat with the adults, waiting for the doors of ministry to open.

Those doors never opened, and MaryAnn asked me to help in children's church. I agreed to just sit with the kids and keep them under control while others were teaching. After a couple of weeks of this, I agreed to help with the puppet ministry—but that was it, I refused to do anything else. After a few more weeks, I found myself helping my wife lead worship, but I insisted that was all I would do. After more time had passed, I was conducting the entire service and loved it! While stationed at Scott, MaryAnn gave birth to our own two children, James and Bethany.

My wife and I continued in children's ministry for 12 years. Our work with children continued even over-seas while we were stationed in the Republic of Turkey.

We had been stationed at Scott AFB for almost three years now and I was getting restless. I wanted to go over-seas. One morning, on my way to work, as I was praying—or should I say, complaining—to the Lord about not getting any orders for an overseas assignment, He spoke to me in my heart: "You told Me you would go anywhere in the world, but you have only volunteered for places like Hawaii and Guam. If you are serious, volunteer worldwide and I will give you an overseas assignment."

"But if I do that," I said to the Lord, "You will send me to Turkey, and MaryAnn doesn't want to go to Turkey."

The Lord replied, "Are you serious about following Me anywhere in the world?" I said, "Yes Lord, but if this is what You want, then when I get to the office I will call MaryAnn and tell her. If she is in agreement, I'll know this is of You and I will volunteer worldwide."

When I got to my office, I called MaryAnn and told her "I think the Lord wants me to volunteer worldwide."

MaryAnn said, "Great, go ahead!"

I said, "But this means we will probably go to Turkey."

She said, "Fine, then let's go!"

I volunteered worldwide later that day, and in three months, we were on our way to Turkey!

We left for Turkey in June 1985. James was only two years old and Bethany was only six months old. MaryAnn and I were going overseas as missionaries, just as the Lord had said to me three years previously. He would have the United States government pay for our expenses while making it possible for us to preach in countries otherwise closed to the gospel!

Turkey is one of those countries where Christianity is illegal. Even though the constitution of Turkey claims freedom of religion, in reality, the true Christian Church of Turkey is publicly persecuted. Evangelical Christians are forced to meet in secret and often harassed by police. Christians there are tortured and jailed simply because they are Christians and for no other reason. At that time, Ankara, Turkey was a city of over four million people in which there were only thirty known Christians in the underground church. I volunteered to go for three years.

When we arrived at our assignment, I discovered I did not have a position in my career field—the Air Force had made a mistake. The position I was filling was for transportation and I was a supply man. I knew God had orchestrated this assignment all the way.

We began our work right away, making contact with as many Christians as we could find both within the military and civilian populations. Through the chapel on the air station, we met some Turks who attended Sunday services on the base—they had obtained a pass from the American security police. With these Turks and others, we started having church meetings in our home, which quickly grew by word of mouth from five people to thirty people.

We had a multinational group of people coming to the meetings. Some were from various countries of Africa. Others were from the Philippines, Iran, America, and of course, Turkey.

Before long, we became close friends with Candan, one of the Turks—a born again and Spirit-filled Christian. She was a student at the university in Ankara. In fact, many of the people in our group came from the university after hearing about our meetings through word of mouth. Candan spoke English and became an interpreter for the other Turks in the meetings. One day, Candan approached us with a personal need—she had no place to live. Since we had an extra bedroom in our apartment, we invited her to live with us, which she did for the next two-and-a-half years or so. Candan became a very big help with shopping for groceries to being our guide around Turkey and babysitting our children.

Stationed on remote communication sites around Turkey were several other young American airmen, who also found their way to our doorstep. They would come down off the remote mountain sites every weekend and stay with us—sometimes as many as four or five at a time.

Three months after our arrival in Turkey, I began to have a greater understanding of what Jesus meant that morning in 1981 when He told me, "You must become a broken man before I can ever use you."

Our office held a good-bye party in August 1985, at a restaurant downtown, for one of the people returning to the U.S. after a tour of duty. Turkey is not a very clean country, and does not have much along the lines of refrigeration, either. August in Turkey is known as the fly season. After the meal I went back to the office to finish out the day, and then went home to our apartment building on the east side of Ankara. That night, I became very ill. I began vomiting and had stomach cramps with diarrhea.

Even though the vomiting had stopped by the next day, the stomach cramps and severe diarrhea continued. After two weeks, I began to notice that urinating was becoming painful and restricted. I had no idea what was going on—the doctors had tried everything to get the diarrhea under control, but nothing worked. A week later, my eyes swelled almost completely shut and were dark red.

The American doctors had no clue what was happening to me, as my body became racked with pain. After another week the swelling in my eyes began to decrease, but then my left knee swelled to the point that I could not bend it. I went to a Turkish doctor who diagnosed my condition as a disease called Reiter's Syndrome.

A week later, my left wrist also swelled up like a balloon. Then all the joints of my body began to swell and become stiff. I was med-evaced (a military term for medically evacuated) to southern Turkey, to a base known as Incirlik Air Force Base, where doctors tried to drain the fluid off my knee. When the doctor told me not to worry because he had done this procedure hundreds of times, I knew I was in for a real treat. After administering a shot of anesthesia to my knee, the doctor brought out this hypodermic needle around three or four inches long. Of course, it looked like it was about six to ten inches long, from my vantage point!

The doctor proceeded to insert the needle into my knee in order to draw out the fluid from around my kneecap. As he did this, he pushed the needle too far and it began to pierce the bone of my leg. I have never felt so much excruciating pain in my life. After this procedure was completed, I was informed that they could not determine anything from the fluid they had taken from my knee. They were going to med-evac me to Wiesbaden, Germany.

At Wiesbaden, the diagnosis of Reiter's Syndrome was confirmed. I was told this disease was incurable. This was only the beginning—from then on, I continued med-evac trips back and forth to Germany as doctors experimented with one drug after another, only to have each attempt fail to bring the disease under control.

Other than administering different medications in an attempt to keep the disease under control, the doctors said there was nothing they could do. Reiter's Syndrome affects many different parts of the body—all joints (especially weight-bearing joints), the prostate gland, urinary tract, muscles, tendons, and ligaments (especially the Achilles tendon), and the lower back, as well as the eyes and the circulatory system.

Reiter's, also called reactive arthritis, is similar to rheumatoid arthritis. It is a very slow, progressive disease, which in extreme cases causes crippling, blindness, urinary tract failure, circulation problems, infections in the prostate, possibly heart attacks and heart defects, among other things.

The way the disease works is rather simple to explain. I inherited an immune system that was sensitive to a certain type of bacteria transmitted by flies. Flies contaminated my food at the Turkish restaurant where the party was held. When the bacteria entered my body, my immune system went crazy and began attacking me instead of the bacteria. Now, even though the bacteria has left my body, my immune system still acts as though the bacteria is still inside me, attacking me continually.

Even though I was very sick, God continued to use me to heal others of various sickness and diseases. It seemed strange to me that God would heal others through me while I remained sick. But the Lord reminded me of something I had heard in Bible college: "the gifts of the Spirit are for helping others, not yourself." That is why we have 1 Corinthians 13 sandwiched between chapters 12 and 14. Love for the people to whom we are ministering is the only motivation for being used by God in the gifts of the Spirit. So, for whatever reason, God began using me to heal our neighbors.

In Turkey, every apartment building has a janitor who is called a Kapici. Our Kapici had a son who had been born with a serious defect in his legs and hips. At the age of four, the Kapici's son was still unable to walk, and doctors said there was no hope for the boy to ever walk without very intensive surgery. Our Kapici did not have enough money to pay for the surgery and did not know where else to turn. Since we were having church meetings in our home, the Kapici knew we were Christians. He told us he could hear us singing and praising God. One morning, our Kapici came to our door, asking us to come and pray for his son. We grabbed some olive oil and followed the man to his apartment where his son was lying on the couch, unable to move. Through Candan, our interpreter, we explained to the boy that we would like to pray for him in the name of Jesus. The boy seemed very excited, and wanted us to begin praying right away. We were not there long—maybe all of about ten minutes. The next day, the boy was out in the yard playing. He had been completely and miraculously healed!

The news of this healing spread like wildfire throughout the apartment building. Some of the Turks who were attending our meetings became fearful about all the publicity. So we tried to keep our worship as quiet as possible, in an effort to not draw attention to ourselves—since, as I have already mentioned, in those days Christianity was illegal.

CHAPTER EIGHT
God is Not a Bubble Gum Machine

I can do all things through Christ who strengthens me.

~Philippians 4:13

Not long after I became desperately ill with Reiter's Syndrome, all my well-meaning Christian brothers and sisters came to comfort me. Of course, each had words of wisdom as to why I was suffering, as well as the perfect combination or procedure for me to follow that guaranteed complete healing.

Some said I was sick because I had sin in my life. Others said that, since I was suffering from an arthritic condition, I must have bitterness in my life—"all I needed to do" was go back to anyone who had hurt me and tell them I forgave them, and I would be healed. Many thought I was sick because I did not have enough faith. I was told "all I needed to do" was to confess only positive statements about my condition—they gave me certain Scripture passages to quote out loud morning, day and night. They said I must never confess anything negative or tell anyone that I was sick.

When none of these ideas worked for me, it was my fault, according to my comforters, that I was not healed. However, God is not a "bubble gum machine," waiting for us to simply put in the right amount of change to make Him give us what we want. I'm sure these dear brothers and sisters in Christ meant well, but now not only was I still sick, I was left with a heavy burden of guilt.

When I prayed about my situation, Jesus always directed me to the same passages of Scripture, one of which is Philippians 4:11–13 where Paul writes,

> *Not that I speak in regard to need, for I have learned in whatever state I am, to be content: I know how to be abased, and I know how to abound. Everywhere and in all things I have learned both to be full and to be hungry, both to abound and to suffer need. I can do all things through Christ who strengthens me.*

"I can do all things" includes failing, losing, becoming sick, poverty, losing a loved one, death, and deprivation. "All things" *means* "all things." Prior to coming down with Reiter's Syndrome, I would read this passage and think of all the good things I could do through Christ who strengthens me—*I can get a high paying job, I can be healthy, I can overcome all my faults and sins*, etc. Now, I can see that "all things" means much more then that. I can also persevere, labor under a heavy load, be patient in the midst of great adversity, praise Jesus and be content with my life in good times and in bad.

In the midst of this great adversity, God's grace was pouring into my spirit, enabling me to come closer to Him and say, "No matter what happens to me, good or bad, I will serve my Lord and praise Him and be content."

Days turned into weeks, weeks turned into months, the months turned into years, but still I was not healed. Everything the doctors tried to control the disease failed. As I mentioned earlier, it was difficult to understand why God continued to use me to heal other people while I remained not only sick but my condition worsened.

We moved, in late 1985, to another apartment building where the other tenants were also American. However, our Kapici was Turkish, and as we began reaching out to him through our Turkish friend, Candan, we discovered his daughter had a birth defect similar to the Kapici of our last building. Candan told us our Kapici had paid the Muslim priest, or *shaykh*, to pray for his daughter to be healed. The Muslim shaykhs prayed but were unsuccessful and said they could do nothing. Doctors, also, had said they could do nothing for the girl, so the Kapici then took her to a witch, who was unable to help the girl either.

Through Candan, my interpreter, I told our Kapici about Jesus Christ and how Jesus could heal his daughter. Our Kapici agreed to let us pray for her and offered to pay me. I refused the money and told him, "Jesus will heal your daughter for free!" My wife and I anointed the girl with oil in the name of Jesus and prayed for her healing. The next day, the little girl was not only walking—for the first time in her life, she was also running! No one could even tell by looking at her that anything had ever been wrong with her! This was truly a miracle of God!

A few months later, the Kapici came to our door early one Saturday morning. Fortunately, Candan was now living with us in our extra bedroom so we were able to understand what our Kapici was trying to tell us. His wife was very sick and he was afraid she might die. He had taken her to the doctor, who had given her medicine, but it didn't work.

He then took his wife to the shaykh and paid him to pray for her, but when their prayers didn't work, the shaykh told our Kapici his wife must have peed in a bad toilet and Satanic spirits had come up into her, so nothing could be done. The Kapici then took his wife to a witch, who was also unable to help. So, now he was coming to us, hoping we would pray for her in the name of Jesus. Again he offered money, but we refused to accept it and told him, "Jesus will heal your wife for free!"

We followed the Kapici to his apartment. When he opened the door, the stench of death was so strong we could hardly breathe. The woman was clearly taking her last breaths before she would die. The Kapici said his wife has been bedridden for weeks, unable to even sponge bathe. We told her we were going to pray for her healing in the name of Jesus Christ. Anointing her with oil, we prayed for her healing in Jesus' name and returned to our apartment.

The next afternoon, our Kapici came to our door with a joyful face. His wife was not only out of bed, she was doing all her regular chores, cleaning the house and cooking! Truly, God performed a miracle! The Kapici was shouting, "praise God Jesus!" And we all rejoiced with him.

About a month later, there was a knock on our front door. It was our Kapici again holding his left arm. He told us his arm was swollen and there was a strange rash all over it. He said, "I didn't go to any doctors, I didn't go to the shaykh, I didn't want to waste my time with any witches. I wanted God Jesus to heal me!" We anointed him with oil and prayed for his healing in the name of Jesus, and then he left with a smile on his face. The next day he came back and showed us his arm, which was completely back to normal—no swelling or rash at all! We rejoiced with him again and gave Jesus all the glory!

In the midst of all these miracles, we were continuing our church services in our home. The Lord poured out His Spirit in those meetings. People received Christ, were baptized in the Holy Spirit, and grew spiritually.

A young Turkish man visited our service one night. The other Turkish believers clammed up and became very quiet. When I later asked Candan why the Turks acted this way, she told us the Turkish Christians were afraid the visitor could have been a member of the Turkish Military Police, whose spies often attended meetings to find out who was present, and turn them over to authorities.

This new Turk claimed to be a student at the university in Ankara. He had heard about our meetings, he claimed, through word of mouth. He continued coming to our meetings for three weeks. After his third visit, I asked him if he knew Jesus as his personal Savior. He told me he believed that Jesus was a great prophet. I responded with, "That's a good start," and left it at that.

Five days later, early on a Sunday morning, we heard knocking at our front door. It was this young Turkish man. He told us he wanted to know Jesus as his personal Savior, but didn't know how to do this. He asked us to help him.

We told him we would love to, and proceeded to lead him to Christ! He left rejoicing.

Through all these wonderful miracles, my health continued to fail. I was transported back and forth to Germany. Doctors tried one drug after another, with no favorable results. The Christian community in Ankara and in America prayed for my healing, but it never came. Whenever I prayed about my situation, the Lord gave me another answer through 2 Corinthians 12:7–10:

And lest I should be exalted above measure by the abundance of the revelations, a thorn in the flesh was given to me, a messenger of Satan to buffet me, lest I be exalted above measure. Concerning this thing I pleaded with the Lord three times that it might depart from me. And He said to me, "My grace is sufficient for you, for my strength is made perfect in weakness." Therefore most gladly I will rather boast in my infirmities, that the power of Christ may rest upon me. Therefore, I take pleasure in infirmities, in reproaches, in needs, in persecutions, in distresses, for Christ's sake. For when I am weak, then I am strong.

God turns our faults and weaknesses into our strengths. Our faults and weaknesses become our strengths because we have to rely more on the Lord in those weak areas of our lives—thus turning bad into good.

And we know that all things work together for good to those who love God, to those who are the called according to His purpose (Rom. 8:28).

CHAPTER NINE
For His Sake

> *Yes, and all who desire to live godly in Christ Jesus will suffer persecution.*
>
> ~2 Timothy 3:12

After our arrival in Turkey and apparent success with our home meetings, I requested permission from the Base Chaplains to conduct Sunday evening Pentecostal church services at the officers' club downtown. After submitting the required credentials, this permission was granted. Previously, Sunday night services had been conducted by the chaplains and had a very low attendance.

Two chaplains were assigned to our air station—one represented the Baptists' beliefs and the other was Episcopalian. Neither chaplain understood the Pentecostal experience and so both publicly taught against it. Every week, chapel was dry, boring, and liturgical. The chaplains proclaimed and advertised an ecumenical service, where everyone could freely express themselves in all ways of worship, but that couldn't have been any farther from the truth. The so-called ecumenical services were either Baptist or Episcopal, depending on which chaplain was conducting the service that week.

At first, things went very well—the service attendance was less than a handful under the chaplains' direction and now was doubled in size. People were excited about the new services where they finally could worship God in the freedom of the Holy Spirit instead of dead religious rituals. As the attendance grew, people began to have salvation experiences. People were baptized in the Holy Spirit. Everything was going great—we were having Sunday night services at the officers club, and during the week, we were conducting church services in our home.

Then, one afternoon, I received a message to report to the chaplain's office. When I arrived, the chaplain, who seemed upset, coldly directed me to sit down. He had been receiving many complaints, he told me, about the way I conducted the Sunday night services. People wanted to return to the old way in which the services had been conducted. I asked how many people had actually complained and the chaplain replied, "Thirty people." When I asked for their names, the chaplain was only able to provide me with two—of people who didn't even attend my services! The chaplain then dropped the pretense and told me he was taking back the Sunday night services.

The attendance on Sunday night dropped from the forties, to five, to sometimes ten on a good night. I received a message from the chaplains' office that the chaplain wanted to see me. When I came into the chaplain's office, he seemed as upset as ever. He had decided, he told me, to give the Sunday night service back to me. Thanking him, I went on my way.

Some people, who were simply unhappy that the Sunday night services were being conducted by a Pentecostal, began to spread rumors that I was not qualified to preach and should be replaced. Those attending one of the adult Sunday school classes were advised by their teacher that I did not have "any real knowledge of the Scriptures." This man spent an entire class trying to prove I was teaching false doctrine. He insisted that there was no Baptism in the Holy Spirit, and speaking in tongues was not for today.

MaryAnn came home one Sunday afternoon as I was preparing for the Sunday night service and told me she had heard a rumor on base that the chaplains gave someone else permission to conduct the service that night. When she told me who it was, I realized it was probably true—the man was the same Sunday school teacher who had expressed publicly, several times, his disagreement with the doctrine of the Baptism of the Holy Spirit. I went to prayer for the rest of the afternoon to decide what to do if he tried to take the service away from me.

That evening, I had barely started the service when this man my wife had warned me about came into the room. Talking very loudly, he disrupted the service, saying he had permission from the chaplain's office to conduct the service himself. I refused, and after ranting and raving for a few minutes, he stopped and sat down. I spoke for a few minutes and then announced my resignation. I then told the man he could have the service.

Many people were upset by this, and attendance at the Sunday night service dropped off once again. From that point onward, I stuck to our midweek home services which grew to the point that we had to move the meeting out of our home. I submitted a request to the chaplains and the base commander's office for permission to meet in one of the rooms in the old hotel downtown. Once used to house newcomers, this hotel, now no longer in use, had some rooms that were large enough to host the large crowds of people who came to our midweek services. The chaplains and the base commander approved our request. The services at the hotel were great— while meeting at the hotel, we baptized five people in a bathtub and had wonderful times of worship and fellowship.

A young airman came in one day, while I was in my office working, and asked if I was Sgt. Terry Barber. "Yes," I replied. He was new on station, he told me, and just had his welcome briefing from one of the chaplains. Part of the chaplain's briefing to newcomers was devoted to warning them to "stay away from Sgt. Terry Barber" he said. "The chaplains are telling everyone you're a troublemaker." Then he commented, "He knew he had to come and meet me, because I was probably 'on fire for God!'" We became good friends.

I determined within myself, through much prayer, that I was not going to let these lies about my character get me down. I would pray for God's help to let me release to Him my desire for a good reputation. These were very difficult days for me, but I continued serving the Lord by His grace.

CHAPTER TEN
The True Measurement of Spirituality

Then Jesus said to His disciples, "If anyone desires to come after Me, let him deny himself, and take up his cross, and follow Me. For whoever desires to save his life will lose it, but whoever loses his life for My sake will find it."

~MATTHEW 16:24–25

During our three years in Turkey, MaryAnn and I also worked with the Turkish underground church. Since the Turkish police did not have access to our military post office box, it provided an ideal means to smuggle Bibles and Christian literature into the country. I even smuggled an entire computer, piece by piece, into the country. The underground church was able to build a mailing list from which to send Christian literature to thousands of addresses in Turkey.

We smuggled clothes and money to the underground church as well. The city of Ankara at that time had a population of over four million people, while the underground church consisted of only approximately thirty people. Some of these dear saints lived in shacks with dirt floors, no electricity, and no running water. Yet, when you looked at them, they appeared to possess all of the riches the world had to offer. Their faces shone with the love and joy that only Jesus could bring.

A German friend I had met at one of the chapel services was in the country as a businessman—but really, he was there for the same reasons we were. He and his wife were missionaries like MaryAnn and I. My friend and I would take hundreds of Christian pamphlets and go out late at night to put these pamphlets in as many mailboxes as we could. On the back of the pamphlets, we wrote a telephone number and address in Germany where interested people could call or write for more information.

One night, we were almost caught as we distributed around 100 pamphlets—but, by the grace of God, we managed to escape. The next day, newspaper headlines read, "What do they want from us?" Full-page pictures of the pamphlets were shown for everyone to read, and the accompanying article tried to make fun of the pamphlets and discredit them. Instead of accomplishing this, the publicity ensured that the pamphlets became known all over the city! Instead of only 100 households reading the pamphlets, thousands of households read them in the newspaper. The German address had a phone ringing off the hook and was inundated with hundreds of letters from people wanting more information about Jesus and how they could have assurance of salvation. What the devil meant for harm, God turned around for good.

In the spring of 1988, as we were starting our preparations to move back to the U.S., another opportunity for spiritual growth came our way. The military legal office notified me that my name was on the Turkish Military

Police most wanted list. My crime was smuggling Bibles and Christian literature into the country and distributing the materials to Turks. The penalty for this crime was seven to ten years in prison.

The Turkish military police obtained my name from one of my contacts with the underground church in Ankara. Arrested and imprisoned for his faith in Christ, my contact had been tortured by the police in order to get more names of other believers. The police placed him in a large tub of ice water and hooked up electrical wires to his testicles. They then administered electric shocks to him until he provided them with the names of other Christians. The police also found my name and address in his phone book, and that is how I was now featured on their most wanted list.

The Air Force decided to get me out of the country before the Turkish military police could arrest me. I was ordered to board a C-9 medical airlift en route to Germany via Spain. The plan was for me to leave my wife and kids in Turkey and meet them in Germany a few weeks later. However, as the plane was taxiing down the runway preparing to take off, the Turks stopped the plane, came on board and seized me. I was certain I had been caught, only to learn my own unit had stopped the plane! Because I was a fugitive of the law, Spain had refused to allow me into their country.

The next plan was to catch a Turkish bus to Incirlik AFB in Adana, Turkey. This would be a ten- to twelve- hour trip over the Tarsus Mountains. The bus was to leave Ankara at 11 p.m. that night. I tried to rejoice through all of this, but I could not—I was scared and very concerned about leaving my family behind. My Christian friends were happy and excited for me because I had been found worthy to be persecuted for the cause of Christ.

That night at the bus station, my wife and kids tried to encourage me through prayer. Bethany, age three, sang to me this song that expresses how we all felt that night, "Cast all your cares upon Him... " With tears we parted, not knowing if we would ever see each other again.

The bus was crowded and full of cigarette smoke, as all Turkish buses are. I found the last available seat, at the back of the bus, and waved good-bye to my family as we started on our way. I tried to settle in for what I knew was going to be a very long journey, overnight through the Tarsus Mountains, to southern Turkey. I wondered if the way I felt was anything like what Paul felt during his various trials. *Now I'm traveling through the same mountains he traveled through several hundred years earlier* flashed through my mind.

The bus made several stops along the way, dropping people off and picking up others, in what looked like the middle of nowhere. Then, around 4 a.m. only halfway to our destination, the bus made another stop. My thought that it was only one more of many routine stops was promptly banished when several Turkish Military Police boarded the bus.

I did not know whether they were looking for me or someone else. The police started checking everyone's identification cards and passports. I pretended I was asleep, and prayed they would not notice me or somehow not ask me for any identification. When they got to me, the policeman woke me up and asked for my identification. Nervously, but trying to act as calm as I could, I handed the policeman my

Military Identification. He peered at the ID for what seemed like hours, and then he looked at me. He looked at the ID and then he looked at me *again*. Then he said something in Turkish to one of the other policemen, and gave back my ID. A few minutes later, the police got off the bus, and we continued on our journey to Adana. I knew the Lord was with me and had protected me from the Turkish police!

We arrived in Adana as the sun was coming up. I got off the bus near the front gate of Incirlik AFB. Even though Incirlik has American forces stationed on it, the base was still a Turkish base, so I walked to the gate exercising care as to whom I talked ,since almost anyone could be working as an informant for the police. After receiving permission to enter the base, I walked about a half mile from the gate to the military hotel.

I checked into my room and tried to call Ankara to check on my family. While the U. S. Embassy had assured me the Turks only wanted *me* and would not try to arrest my wife and children, I was still very concerned for their safety, since the embassy also informed us the police, in order to get more evidence against me and also to find out where I was hiding, had probably placed a tap on our phone. Because of this, my wife and I had devised some key phrases so that we could tell how everyone was doing and if any other news had come concerning our situation with the police. After I had made certain my wife and children were all right, I settled down to get some rest.

After almost two weeks of hiding, I received a message from my office in Ankara that my name had mysteriously disappeared from the most wanted list. Neither the U.S. Embassy nor the military legal office gave any logical explanation for this disappearance. I knew in my heart that God pulled out His big, supernatural eraser and erased my name from the list! I went home to be reunited with my family in Ankara, finished my tour of duty in Turkey as originally planned, and returned to the States with my family!

As for my Turkish contact with the underground church, he was released from police custody and never formally charged with a crime. Later, the police sent an informant into one of the church services of the underground church and my friend was arrested again—this time, with three of his friends. Somehow, a mistake led to the informant's being arrested also.

All four men were sent to solitary confinement without ever being officially charged with a crime. They were placed in a room with no windows, in complete darkness for a month. During that time, my contact and his Christian friends worshiped and sang songs of praise to Jesus! The informant, arrested by mistake, was going nuts, screaming and crying for help. When the men emerged from solitary confinement, they were stronger in their faith than they had ever been before, and witnessed to all the other prisoners. Revival broke out within the prison and many prisoners received Christ as their personal Savior. Soon after that, my contact and his friends were released.

CHAPTER ELEVEN

Grow Where You're Planted!

And whatever you do, do it heartily, as to the Lord and not to men, knowing that from the Lord you will receive the reward of the inheritance; for you serve the Lord Christ.

~COLOSSIANS 3:23–24

We arrived in the States June 3, 1988. The trip was not the greatest. We were delayed in Geneva and consequently missed our connecting flight in New York. We had to sleep in the airport because we couldn't afford a hotel. Finally, however, we arrived at my mother's home in Ohio, very tired and irritated, but very glad to be back in America where we could go to church and not have to be concerned about the secret police breaking in and taking us to jail.

Our next assignment was at Griffiss AFB, in Rome, New York. After taking a month off visiting relatives in Ohio and Long Island, we began the next chapter of our lives at Griffiss, looking for a house and a church to call home.

I wanted a large church where there would be plenty of ministry opportunities, and MaryAnn wanted a small church where we could build relationships. The first church we visited was rather large, and I had been praying that I would not have to wait a long time for ministry—however, the pastor hardly gave me the time of day, let alone permitted me to get involved in any ministry. We found a mobile home for sale on two acres of land, out in the middle of nowhere, in a very small crossroads of a town called Florence. My wife looked in the phone book and found a church in Camden, another small town, about five miles away.

We visited the church that Sunday night. It met in the local Grange building, which also served as a meeting place for many other community activities. We arrived late and couldn't help disturbing the meeting since there was just a handful of people there, anyway. We sat down and began worshiping the Lord; all of a sudden, we could sense the presence of the Lord in that building in a very strong and special way. As the service progressed, the pastor asked if we would like to testify. I stood up and began to tell of some of the persecution and trouble we had experienced in Turkey, and how we were tremendously thankful to be back in the States where we could worship freely without fear.

After the service, the pastor invited us to his home for ice cream. We accepted the invitation, and as we were fellowshipping, the pastor shared with us how, earlier in the day, he read a magazine article about Turkey and some of the persecution going on there. He shared how the testimony I had given was the exact same testimony he had read about earlier that day!

There are no coincidences with God; He had orchestrated our meeting this pastor. A couple of weeks later, the pastor had to be out of town, and he asked me to conduct the church services while he was gone. Praise God! I did not have to wait a long time for ministry opportunities, and the church was small enough for my wife as well.

As time passed, we became heavily involved with the church in Camden as members and serving as children's church coordinators. After the first year, I became a deacon, and then youth pastor and associate pastor. Then I began seeking official credentials for ministry, receiving my official license to preach on April 26, 1990, which was also my birthday.

From 1987 to 1989, the Reiter's Syndrome had gone into remission and I was able to do any physical activity I wanted. However, in late 1989, the disease became active again and I began having severe flare-ups which kept me going back and forth between hospital and doctor's appointments.

In 1990, MaryAnn and I started a Christian youth center I called "The Cornerstone." Along with diversions such as pool, ping-pong tables, and air hockey tables, we had local Christian bands performing concerts and preaching the gospel. I had finally seen the fulfillment of my street ministry vision from back in Mount Gilead, Ohio! Many young people received Jesus as their personal Savior. Other youth groups from neighboring cities came to the youth center to minister in skits and preaching, and we organized our own ministry group from our church to do the same. We were very busy people. Remember, during all this, I was still working full time in the Air Force!

We lived about forty miles from the base, so I spent a lot of time driving back and forth in my van between my house and the base. During winter months it was especially challenging, since we lived right smack in the middle of a snow belt, and I don't mean the kind of belt you put around your waist, either! When we first arrived in upstate New York, I thought I knew what it was like to live in a place that receives a lot of snow each year. I didn't have a clue what was in store for us. Lake effect snow and snow squalls were terms I had never heard of before. But then, I hadn't heard of whiteouts either, when it snowed so hard you couldn't see your hand in front of your face!

I soon discovered we could get several feet of snow in just a few hours when a snow squall passed through. Most people shovel snow out of their driveway—we had to shovel snow *off our roof* where the snow accumulated so heavily that it would get higher than our chimney and smother out our furnace!

It was an interesting phenomenon, however, that I never had any difficulty driving home from work until I arrived home and pulled into my driveway on Friday afternoon—not Monday or Wednesday, or any other day of the week—only Friday, when I was so tired from the long week and all I wanted to do was to get home and relax with MaryAnn and the kids. It never failed—just as I pulled into my driveway, I would slide and get miserably stuck in my own yard! It always took several hours trying to get unstuck, too!

One weekend was especially challenging—I will never forget it! It was Friday night and as usual, I was stuck in my driveway. I had decided I wasn't going to lose my cool this time, so before I could start getting angry over the situation, I started singing a little song to help me stay calm. It's a song I learned to use whenever I felt myself getting emotionally stimulated in situations like these. The song went like this:

> *Halleluiah anyhow!*
> *Never-never let your troubles*
> *get you down-down-down*
> *but when life's problems come your way*
> *just lift your head up high and say*
> *halleluiah anyhow!*

Depending on how angry I was, the last "halleluiah" would get louder and more emotional. Anyway, this particular night I was already getting rather loud with my song—and I hadn't even started trying to shovel my way *out* yet!

I got out of my van, went to my garage to get a snow shovel, and began shoveling the snow, singing this song the whole time, while a snow squall busily dumped snow on top of me. It was already dark—the sun had gone down about thirty minutes before I began to shovel out my van. Over and over again, I shoved the shovel into the snow and threw the snow over the snow bank, as I continued to sing and the snow squall did "its thing."

Then the unexpected happened—as I threw a shovelful of snow and brought the shovel back to get another load, I noticed my shovel was extremely light, much lighter than previously. All I had was a shovel *handle*. The shovel itself had broken off from the handle and was stuck in the snow bank. Needless to say, as I decided very quickly to go to plan "B," (applying the tire chains), my rendition of "Halleluiah anyhow" became a lot louder and more emotional!

After pulling the tire chains out of the back of the van, I crawled under the van and attached them to the rear tires. I got in the van and started the engine, while I continued serenading the snow squall. I put my foot on the gas and started slowly backing out of the snowdrift. Everything seemed to be going well when suddenly I heard a crashing and scraping noise that sounded like metal-to-metal. The van stopped moving and just sat there with its tires spinning around. I turned off the engine and got out to see what had happened, of course *still* singing, when I saw that both chains had broken and both rear tires were now flat!

I screamed, "HALLELUIAH ANYHOW!" and threw my hat up in the air, jumped into the snowdrift, and lay there kicking and screaming. The neighbors' lights came on as I lay there in the snow. Then I just got quiet, sweating and thinking if only my parishioners could see me now!

As I lay there, thinking how I really blew it this time, I wondered how could God love a person like me. *I will never be what God wants me to be. I'm just a big hypocrite.* Then I noticed little snowflakes landing on my half-bald head, and then another landed on my nose. I began thinking about how there are millions of these little snowflakes and not one of them is exactly alike. They are all different, just as we humans are unique and different from each other. Yet, just as God took the time to make these insignificant tiny snowflakes, how much more care and time did He give in making each of us?

Then the Lord reminded me of the sparrow—how He provides and cares for it from day to day, how much more does He care for me and watch over me... And not only me, but every individual person all around the world. Suddenly, the fact that my van was stuck in the snow with two flat tires was not very important anymore. I realized how meaningless all this really was, not worth all the energy, and I

Grow Where You're Planted!

began to pray as I lay there in the snow, asking for forgiveness for my childish display of anger.

Then, as I continued to lie there in the snow, another snowflake came floating down and landed on my nose, and the Lord began speaking to me about His love for me. He reminded me that among the millions upon millions of people in the world, my Heavenly Father knows me better than I know myself and is interested in me. The Lord also assured me that He does not expect me to live this life alone—He wants to be with me and give me the grace I need to stand and be the person He wants me to be, not in my own strength, in His strength!

The Air Force had moved us three times in the past nine years—from Texas to Illinois, from Illinois to Turkey, and from Turkey to Rome, New York. In all that moving, no matter what life threw at us along the way, the Lord never failed us. The Lord was always there for us, forever faithful, meeting our every need, always true to His Word.

I decided to give up on the van and went in the house for the night to enjoy the blessings of my Lord, a beautiful wife, and wonderful children. As we cuddled up next to each other in our warm, loving home, nothing else mattered anymore. We had each other and we had God, and that was enough. It could storm outside all it wanted to, we were safe and secure from all alarm, and God was still on the throne!

CHAPTER TWELVE

Ask and Ye Shall Receive

> *So Gideon said to God, "If You will save Israel by my hand as You have said—look, I shall put a fleece of wool on the threshing floor; if there is dew on the fleece only, and it is dry on all the ground, then I shall know that You will save Israel by my hand, as You have said."*
>
> ~JUDGES 6:36–37

The Gulf War started in August 1990. My unit was sent overseas to support the B-52 bombers. Because my feet had become severely disfigured from the effects of Reiter's Syndrome, and walking on the cement floors of the supply warehouse had caused me to suffer fallen arches, I had to have surgery on both feet. This for the most part kept me out of the war. I remained at Griffiss, where I supported the war effort by managing chemical warfare equipment and mobility gear for the entire base population of around 8,000 military personnel.

This was no small task, when you consider that we didn't have 8,000 chemical and mobility kits *assembled* at the start of the war. In fact, we didn't have 100! What we *did* have was just stuffed in a closet out of the way. We didn't have the necessary supplies to build the kits, either. Fortunately, after coming on line as the Non-Commissioned Officer in Charge (NCOIC), I began the task of designing a warehouse from which to work. This included everything from painting lines on the floor, to locating and building shelving, to appointing office space.

After ordering as much of the supplies as I could with the amount of money allocated to my section, I decided to go to the base salvage yard. At the salvage yard, I found hundreds of thousands of dollars' worth of mobility equipment, in good—even excellent—condition. Much of it was still sealed in its original packaging. The Army at Fort Drum was getting replacement equipment and shipped the old equipment to salvage. I obtained the equipment at no additional cost to the Air Force! My unit, including myself on crutches, worked sixteen to eighteen hours a day, seven days a week for most of the war, building and issuing out chemical and mobility bags to people as they were deploying overseas. I divided my people into shifts so the office was open around the clock. At the end of the war, I received the Air Force Accommodation Medal for my efforts!

In April 1991, I was sent on another med-evac trip to a hospital in Washington, D.C., this time for kidney problems. The doctors were not sure if Reiter's Syndrome was itself damaging my kidneys or if the Non-steroidal-Anti-Inflammatory (NSAID) drugs they had prescribed to control the Reiter's were damaging my kidneys. When I arrived in Washington, I started having dizzy spells and nausea. The doctor checked my blood pressure the next day and became very alarmed—it was dangerously high, 160 over 110. The doctor directed me to lie down, and after waiting fifteen minutes, she checked my blood pressure again. This time, my pressure was 170 over 115! The doctor called in another doctor, who checked my pressure again. *Now* my pressure was 180 over 120. The doctors became frantic over the situation. I think they were afraid I might explode at any minute. Once I was admitted into the hospital, the doctor started a regimen of blood pressure medications immediately.

I stayed in the hospital for around a week. The doctor released me and sent me back to New York once my blood pressure had stabilized. The cause of the kidney problems was still not clear, but the doctors were leaning towards the opinion that medication was the culprit. Since I needed to be on the medication to help control the Reiter's, the doctors continued it anyway for the time being.

In May of 1991, the Air Force began proceedings to have me discharged, citing my diminishing fitness for military service. I began seeking confirmation from God, asking Him to show me what He wanted me to do concerning this discharge. "If it is Your will for me to get out of the Air Force," I prayed to Him, "then confirm this by providing a way for me to pay off the loan we have on our land, since we will be definitely having financial problems if I get out of the service." A few days later, I got a phone call from my Mother. She told me that my Dad left me some money when he died, and she was going to send it to me. The amount was $10,000. We paid off the land and had some left over.

The Air Force offered me thirty thousand dollars to accept a medical discharge, after which they would have no further obligations to me. I refused—I would spend more than that on medications alone in just one year. There was no way I was about to let them off the hook that easily. Then, I asked the Lord, if He really wanted me out of the service, would He confirm it by causing the Air Force to give me a medical retirement instead of just a medical discharge so I could have retirement benefits? A few weeks later, the Air Force sent me to Texas to be evaluated by a medical board.

My Air Force doctor was required to write an evaluation of my health for the medical board to review. He asked me what I wanted—to stay on active duty or to get out of the military? I hesitated. I knew how the system worked— whatever I wanted, they would give me the opposite. Believing that God wanted me out of the service, by faith I responded, "I want to stay on active duty," knowing that the doctor would do the opposite. I was right. The doctor wrote a recommendation for medical retirement. He said that due to my failing health, I was not worldwide capable, and therefore unfit for military service. Their decision was a medical retirement at forty percent disability—just as I had prayed!

Then I went to the Lord in prayer once again, asking Him to confirm He wanted me out of the Air Force by opening the doors of ministry to me. I didn't want to have to wait a long time for ministry opportunity. A few days later I answered a phone call from the New York District office, asking me if I was interested in taking the pastorate of a small, inner city church in Syracuse, New York. I said yes, and they agreed to send my resume to the church board for consideration.

My medical retirement was effective on July 21, 1991. That evening I was interviewed by the church board for the pastorate position. Following the interview, I left for a month's vacation with my family, during which I prayed about the church in Syracuse. The Lord spoke to me in the Spirit, telling me, "The church has chosen someone else for the position. But don't worry—it won't work out, and they will come back to you." The day I returned from my vacation, I received a phone call from the church wanting me to come and candidate for the pastorate that weekend so the church body could decide if I was the right man for the position. When I arrived, I discovered that they had chosen someone else, but he turned them down—causing them to come back to me, just as the Lord had told me while on vacation!

I was voted in as pastor of the church on September 8, 1991, and on October 1 moved into the parsonage. The Lord provided a renter for our property in Florence. The Lord was clearly in control!

CHAPTER THIRTEEN
Go Into All the World and Preach

"Go therefore and make disciples of all the nations, baptizing them in the name of the Father and of the Son, and of the Holy Spirit, "teaching them to observe all things that I have commanded you; and lo, I am with you always, even to the end of the age." Amen .

~Matthew 28:19–20

MaryAnn and I were excited about what God was doing in our lives. We were filled with expectation for what He had in store for us as pastors of our first church. A lot of hard work awaited us—the church consisted of eighteen members with an average attendance of thirty on Sunday morning. The finances of the church were a shambles, with six or seven thousand dollars in unpaid, overdue bills. The day we moved into the parsonage, the phone company announced they were turning off our phone until the bill was paid.

We spent a lot of time in prayer in those days, seeking the Lord for wisdom in our managment of the church. First, with concurrence from the church board and membership, we took the building fund of over $13,000 and began paying off all the unpaid bills. We had the roof of the parsonage replaced, since it was in very bad condition. Then we began teaching the people personal evangelism. I also began personally interviewing members, to find out more about them and where they fit into the church body. In December 1991 we began "Operation Visitation," visiting each first time visitor of our church in his or her home. We had our first three new converts in just a matter of a week, and by the end of our first year as pastors of the church, we had around thirty-six new converts! The church had grown from eighteen members to thirty, and our average attendance on Sunday morning grew into the forties.

All this time my health continued to slowly worsen. It was now necessary for me to lie down in the afternoons. The doctors offered no relief—if anything, they were confounded by their inability to control the disease's progression. A strong compassion for disabled persons and the elderly had been developed within me by the Lord as I dealt with the disabling effects of Reiter's Syndrome.

Being in the inner city, many people lived on fixed incomes as I did. The church was able to provide us with housing, but was not able to afford to pay me a salary—consequently, we lived off of what the VA paid me in disability payments (a little over seven hundred dollars a month). The Lord was faithful—we did not starve. When necessary, members of other churches in the area stopped by, right when things were getting desperate, and give us food. Also, from time to time, our church was able to give us a small salary of fifty to one hundred dollars a week just when we really needed it. For these reasons it seemed the Lord brought us His poor, elderly, and disabled people to minister to and love.

In 1992, we saw around twenty-five conversions to faith in Christ, and in 1993, around twenty conversions. Not many of these new converts were actually added, however, to the church. Due to my continued failing health, I was unable to follow up with and disciple the people as I should have. On May 11th, 1993, I completed my religious training through correspondence and finally achieved ordained minister status—an accomplishment I thought I would never attain!

In 1994, I declared war on the devil and began my strongest effort yet in evangelism. I had been working for two years at changing the church from a program-centered church to a cell, or small group-centered church, delegating as much of the work as I could to the leaders of each group.

Around this time, a family in our church needed a van desperately. MaryAnn and I decided to give them our van, free of charge. They had three small children and were experiencing serious marital problems. Shortly afterward, the family left our church, and we had no idea where they were. A year later, we were in desperate need of a van to transport people to church services. I began praying on a Tuesday, asking God to put it upon the husband's heart to give us back our van. On Thursday that same week, I received a phone call from the husband. He told me they did not need the van any more, and wanted to know if we would like to have it back! I said, "Yes!" The husband told me later that he was going to sell the van, but his wife insisted he gave it back to me. At the time, they were not even living for the Lord.

In 1994, we had around fifty new converts, and in 1995, we saw around eighty new converts with the help of the distribution of the "Jesus" video in the neighborhoods around the church. By the end of 1995, we had ten small groups meeting at various times and days throughout the week, averaging six to ten adults in a group.

Even though we were finally making some positive headway, I was still desperate for workers—especially in the area of Youth Ministry. For several years, I had been going to a copy store for various administrative support, and had befriended one of the workers there. He started helping me with a few Youth Ministry outreach projects, and eventually started helping me with the Youth Group. Even though he was not a member of my church, and his wife didn't want anything to do with our church, I went ahead and allowed him to help out because we desperately needed the help. A pastor of a small church has a difficult enough time finding help, so when help comes along, we tend to bend the rules as is necessary to make things happen. Another person who had expressed interest in the youth was a married woman. I went ahead with allowing her to work with my friend from the copy store.

As time went on, I got a call from my youth workers requesting a counseling session. When they arrived, they told me they were starting to develop a close relationship with one another and wanted advice on how to guard against allowing their relationship to grow any further. They also said they did not want to end their friendship or stop working together in the youth ministry.

I told them not to put themselves in a position of temptation—"Never allow yourselves to be alone together. Include your spouses in the relationship." Unfortunately, they didn't follow my advice. In the weeks to follow, in spite my continual follow-up work with them, things got worse. As I continued to meet with them, they both assured me the relationship had not progressed and that they had not slept together. However, one night, I received a phone call from one of the relatives of the parties involved. The relative was very concerned about the situation and asked me if I knew my youth workers were sleeping together. I refused to believe it, and called my youth workers to set up another meeting at which I asked them outright if they had been having sex. "No," they responded, "But we have come very close to it." I told them they had to break off their relationship immediately, and one of them would have to leave the youth ministry. They agreed to this. However, they were lying to me—they *had* already had sex.

What happened next was probably my darkest hour as a pastor. I took both of them to their respective spouses to get this problem out in the open. The wife of the copy store worker went absolutely nuts! She started cursing me up one side and down the other. She blamed me and my church for what had happened, and threw us all out of the house. The husband of the woman involved was willing to allow his wife to stay with him—but she was not willing to stay with her husband.

The two youth leaders ran away together, leaving me to pick up the pieces. The next task was telling the rest of the church body what had happened. Eventually, the couple returned home. The woman left for her parents home out west, and the man tried to get his wife to take him back which, eventually, she did. The last time I saw the husband of the female youth leader, he had gotten a divorce and was seeing another woman.

In the spring of 1996, we prepared for another great evangelistic thrust into the heart of the inner city, when I was awakened at 5 a.m. on April 11 with a heart attack. I felt like a heavy weight had been placed on my chest. A sharp pain then shot from the center of my chest, went down my left arm and up the back of my neck, to the top of my head. I told MaryAnn, "Something weird is happening to me—I think I'm having a heart attack. Do you think I should go to the hospital?" She said yes, we got ourselves together, and she drove me to the hospital.

When we arrived at the emergency room, the doctors started running ECGs and taking blood. All the tests came back normal! My doctor was about to send me home, when she saw the look of fear on my face. She decided to look at the ECGs again, and this time noticed a small glitch at the end of one of the ECGs. A cardiologist was summoned to look at the ECG. The cardiologist recommended a heart cauterization the next day to find out for sure what was going on.

The heart cauterization revealed four blocked arteries—three were 90 percent blocked and a fourth was 50 percent blocked. I went into shock at this news and my vital signs dropped to next to nothing, causing cardiac arrest. All I remember after that is doctors and nurses shouting instructions, my bed being turned up in the air so that I was standing on my head, and the cardiologist yelling at me to not wimp out on him as they injected drugs into my IV.

Later, I was moved to intensive care where I could be observed more closely and it was decided I would undergo bypass surgery on Monday, April 15. On the Saturday afternoon before the surgery, MaryAnn decided to go home to get some rest and check on the kids, who were with a family from our church. I was praying and crying out to God for help, pleading with Him not to let me die. I asked Him to let me see my kids grow up and to see my grandkids. About an hour later, I had another bad angina attack, of which I do not remember much except sitting up in bed clinching my chest and doctors scurrying around me. And then I had what I think was an out-of-body experience. I remember floating and looking down at myself in the bed and seeing all the doctors and nurses running about working on me and then everything went dark.

The next thing I remember, I was back in my bed and MaryAnn was following me down a long hallway. My cardiologist had called MaryAnn and told her we were out of time—I would have to undergo emergency bypass heart surgery, so she should return to the hospital immediately. When MaryAnn arrived, with her consent, the decision was to do double bypass surgery. The cardiologist notified the emergency surgery team to come into the hospital. Going down the corridor to the operating room was the last thing I remember about that night.

The operation began at 6 p.m. and continued until after midnight. A major complication occurred with the intubation procedure. Since the bones of my neck had suffered destruction from arthritis, the doctors were unable to get my head back far enough to insert the breathing tube. It took them over two hours and required special equipment and procedures so rarely used that I have to carry instructions around now in my wallet in case I require surgery in the future.

Many people called a local radio station to ask for prayer for me during this time. It was announced on the air for every church to pray for me all across the city. The Lord's grace prevailed, and I survived the surgery. The days and weeks of recovery were the worst days of my life, with much suffering and respiratory complications when my lungs filled with fluid, making it difficult to breathe.

After several trips to the emergency room and several days on water pills, the doctors decided to insert a long needle in my back, passing between my ribs and into my lungs, to drain the water off of them. The first attempt was unsuccessful; they had gone in too high, entering the lung above the water level. The second attempt was successful, draining large amounts of water. Without anesthesia, the procedure was very painful—especially when the needle was passing between my ribs. However, the Lord was with me and got me through these difficult days as well. A few days after coming home from the hospital, one of the people of my church called me and told me it was because I had no faith that all this had happened to me. I thanked him and said goodbye.

CHAPTER FOURTEEN
Know When to Go

For we walk by faith, not by sight.

~2 Corinthians 5:7

My wife and I felt that soon we would have to leave Syracuse and move to the southwest where, hopefully, the milder weather would improve my health. I had also had a burden for Native Americans for some time. I felt that perhaps—although I did not see how this could ever be possible—I could do some missionary work on the reservations.

In July 1996, we took a month off from the church and went to Ohio to visit my family. My mother owned some property in southern New Mexico that she said she would give us, if we wanted it. MaryAnn was exhausted from all the stress we had been under, so she stayed in Ohio to rest while James and Bethany flew to Florida to visit my sister. My brother, Randy, and I drove out west to spy out the land for the possibility of moving there next year.

The trip was long, hot, and challenging, since I was still recovering from the heart surgery. After visiting the Grand Canyon and driving through Arizona, we had to make an emergency stop in Tucson to have the brakes on our Chevy Astro repaired. Then we swung east again to New Mexico to check my mother's property. I gathered as much information as I could about the area—hospitals, schools, and what it would cost to upgrade my mother's vacant lot into adequate housing for our family. We then took off for Ohio again. The trip took about three weeks. When we arrived in LaRue, Ohio, we were tired and ready for a home-cooked meal.

The following Sunday, MaryAnn and I went with my mother to her church in Marion, Ohio. At the end of the refreshing service, the Pastor prophesied over MaryAnn and me that we had been considering moving to the southwest and that the Lord was with us in this move. Also, he continued, the Lord would work out all the details in answer to my wondering about missions work there. MaryAnn and I could not believe our ears. As we walked to the car, I asked my mother if she had told the pastor about our situation prior to this service. She said she had not told him anything at all, and was just as amazed as we were.

A few days later, we left Ohio to go home to Syracuse, New York. I prayed the Lord to give us confirmation concerning our move to New Mexico, and MaryAnn and I made travel plans to go down to Deming in October. There were four things that were going to have to be taken care of first, I told the Lord, if He really wanted us to resign the pastorate in Syracuse and move to the southwest. Number one—since our church was being evicted from its present meeting place, we needed a new building to conduct church services. Number two—we needed to sell the property and mobile home in Camden, New York, that we were presently renting out. Number three—my claim for disability compensation that I had been fighting for four years now needed to be resolved. Number four—I had around $60,000 in hospital bills from my heart surgery that needed to be paid before I could even think about moving.

We arrived home in late July. A few days later, I received a phone call from a realtor with whom I had been working concerning a warehouse. We had been interested in the warehouse, but unable to raise enough money to buy it, and could not afford to rent. I had not heard from him for a couple of months, and was rather surprised to hear from him now, especially concerning this building.

The owners were adamant about the price and about how much they wanted for rent. He asked if we were still interested in the warehouse and I said yes, but added that we couldn't afford it. He wanted to know, would we be interested in renting the building at $1500 a month? I said we were interested in renting the building, but could not afford to pay that much each month. He asked what we could afford, to which I replied, "The highest we could go is eight hundred dollars a month." He said he would talk to the owners of the building and get back to me. About thirty minutes later, the realtor called back and said the owner had agreed to our offer of eight hundred dollars a month and we could move in on the first of August!

A few days later, my wife and I went up to Camden to put our property on the market through a local realtor. We had tried to sell the property before on our own, but were unsuccessful. The people looking at the property only wanted to rent, not buy, and the last renters had trashed the property. Ten days after we had placed the property in the realtor's hands, however, we had a buyer for the property. The realtor was amazed at how quickly this took place. she had told us property like ours always takes a long time to sell, and sometimes never sells.

At the same time, I received a letter from the VA in Buffalo that I had won my claim for disability compensation and there would be over $25,000 in retroactive compensation coming to me on August 1. MaryAnn and I then applied for a grant we had heard about at the hospital in hope that we could possibly get our hospital debt reduced. The hospital told us if we didn't qualify for Medicaid, we could apply for the grant. We went to the Medicaid office, but since we owned a car, we didn't qualify for Medicaid. We submitted the paperwork for the grant, and a few weeks later, received a letter from the hospital. My debt had been completely *paid in full*! In fact, for several months afterward, we received checks in the mail for hundreds of dollars in reimbursements from past medical bills we had paid! Praise God! I think the Lord was trying to tell us to move to the southwest—what do you think?

The first Sunday of August 1996, I announced my resignation to the church. One brother was so upset he went out into the parking lot and threw up! It was very hard for us to leave, but we knew we had to go and that holding on would help neither the church nor us.

The church let us stay in the parsonage until we were able to make housing arrangements elsewhere. This was a big help, since we did not have anywhere to go yet. We decided against moving to Deming because the closest adequate medical care was over fifty miles away in Las Cruces, New Mexico. So we decided to check out Las Cruces but we were unable to get much information about the city or real estate in the area. What we did receive, we did not like. Then we received a letter from one of our old Air Force friends who had just received our annual mass-mailing of family news. We thought they were in Louisiana, but they had moved to Tucson, Arizona and our letter had been forwarded to them there.

Our friend said, "What about Tucson? We've been here for a few months now and love it." We decided to check it out for ourselves. I remembered that during my earlier trip out west with my brother, we'd had to stop for brake repairs on the van while passing through Tucson. Waiting for my brake repairs, I had picked up a list of real estate information about Tucson. We chose three realtors out of a long list and called each one. Within a few short days, all kinds of information came flooding in on real estate, schools, hospitals, etc. MaryAnn and I changed our travel plans for New Mexico to Tucson, and pushed them up from October to September.

We arrived in Tucson in early September and met with our real-estate agent the next morning. Our real-estate agent had a list of over thirty houses for us to look at which met our list of requirements—including location and school district. (One of my requirements for the house was a large saguaro cactus in the front yard.) We chose the fourth house we looked at, submitted a purchase offer, and it was accepted. Our real-estate agent was amazed at how easy everything was going. For example, the house was not supposed to be on the market any longer—he thought the house had already been sold weeks before, since it was not on any of the computer listings, but there it was waiting for us—compliments of the Lord Jesus!

We flew back to Syracuse to start getting our things together for our move in early October. The moving van came to pick up all our stuff and we were to leave the next morning. The house was completely empty—we slept that night on the floor. Then we received a phone call from the loan officer, telling us our loan had been disapproved. The house in Tucson was not going to be ours.

Here we were in an empty house. Our stuff was already well on its way to Tucson, and we were leaving in the morning but had no place to live when we got there! MaryAnn and I did not know what to do. Was the Lord trying to tell us something? Up until now everything had been going very smoothly, without any problems whatsoever. We decided to go to Tucson, anyway, so we packed the van and left Syracuse the next morning. We both felt this was just a test from the Lord and we were just going to trust Him and take one step at a time. Our next stop was LaRue, Ohio, where my mother and stepfather lived.

We stayed in LaRue a few days while we tried to sort out what was going on and what our plan of action would be once we arrived in Tucson. We thought we would try to get an apartment to live in until we could buy our house, but then discovered apartments cost nine hundred dollars and up a month. We started praying with my parents and we all felt strongly that this was a test from the Lord. He really *did* want us in Tucson and in that house we were attempting to buy.

As we continued to pray, my stepfather declared that the Lord wanted him to loan us the money we needed to buy the house, at the same interest rate we would have gotten from the mortgage company! My stepfather made the arrangements the next day to have the money waiting for us in our bank account when we arrived in Tucson. We moved into our new home in mid-October, 1996. Praise the Lord! He is faithful!

CHAPTER FIFTEEN
Whom the Lord Loves He Chastens

> *"My son, do not despise the chastening of the Lord,
> nor be discouraged when you are rebuked by Him;
> For whom the Lord loves He chastens,
> and scourges every son whom He receives."*
>
> ~Hebrews 12:5–6

Soon after moving into our new home, we began our search for the church in which God wanted us to plant ourselves. Retirement from the Air Force made another resource available to us in Davis-Monthan AFB, just a few miles from our home. In the base newspaper, we found an advertisement for a church not too far from the main gate. When we decided to check it out, we discovered the church had a great youth ministry for our kids. We soon started calling this church our home.

The church was wonderful, the worship was powerful, the preaching was good, and the people seemed sincerely interested in being part of our extended family. We were in love with the church and I wanted desperately to get involved in ministry as quickly as possible.

MaryAnn had her doubts and concerns about jumping back into ministry right away. She felt we should take some time to recuperate from the stress and pressures of pastoral life, not to mention my near death experience. I wanted to establish myself in our denominational circles and begin working in evangelistic ministry as the Lord had showed us before we left New York.

While I was still struggling with health problems and not physically able to be in full-time ministry, I was obsessed with the desire to be back in ministry again. I was doing everything in my power to put myself there as soon as possible. God kept saying, "Wait," and I kept walking into every closed door known to man, yet I refused to give up.

At first, I thought I should pursue missions work with the native Americans, and met with the District Superintendent of our denomination. That didn't work out well, unless we were willing to sell the house we'd just bought and move to one of the reservations. He did, however, give us some good advice: "take this opportunity God has given you to minister to your children while they are still young." MaryAnn took it to heart, but I didn't want to hear it.

Then I decided to become a self-proclaimed evangelist. I had some business cards done up and started advertising myself at pastor meetings as an evangelist looking for the opportunity to minister in any church that would have me. I even told people I would preach in their church for free—I just wanted to be a blessing to them!

After about six months and only one invitation for a Sunday night service that didn't go well, I was left very frustrated. For the most part, the pastors in the Arizona district ignored me, both on a personal and professional basis.

Meanwhile, back at my home church in Tucson, by offering to organize and manage a "small group ministry" (more widely known as "cell group"), I found a way to feel useful. Even though the senior pastor was reluctant to allow this kind of ministry in his church, he gave us permission to continue. Little did I know God was about to spank me harder than I have ever been spanked in my entire spiritual life. The true meaning of "becoming a broken man" before God could ever use me was about to be realized.

Surprisingly, God blessed our efforts in the cell group ministry. In only three months, reaching out to only first-time visitors, the cell groups grew to over thirty adults in three groups of ten. The senior pastor was impressed and I was very proud of my accomplishments! The senior pastor was so impressed, in fact, that he invited MaryAnn and I to come on board as staff members heading up the children's ministry of the church. Since the church was very large, around eight hundred people, this was no small job offer and it came with a salary. Needless to say, MaryAnn and I were excited about the offer and went to prayer immediately—only to find God was completely silent on the subject. In the past, MaryAnn and I have always been able to hear God's voice on matters such as this, but for some reason, God was not talking to us. This should have been a red flag that maybe we should not take the position, but since I was lifted up in pride and we felt that the pastor had certainly been praying about this before asking us, we decided to accept.

We were on the job two weeks when the pastor asked me to preach at a Wednesday evening service he was not going to be attending. That week I had been very sick from a Reiter's flare-up, but decided to tough it out and preach anyway. I had a very difficult time delivering the message and knew from responses and facial expressions that my message had not been received well. One of the associate pastors called me the next day complaining about the message I had preached. He then complained to the senior pastor. The senior pastor listened to the tape and called me into his office. He leveled several accusations against me—that my message was an effort to undermine his pastoral authority, that in it I attacked one of the other associate pastors, that I was badgering the people, and the doctrine I was preaching was inaccurate. He then fired me on the spot!

Of course, my world came crashing down all around me. I hugged the man and asked him to forgive me. There was nothing I could have said that would have changed his mind. He had already decided he was accurate in his assumptions and accusations, since he fired me before giving me a chance to defend myself. I *did* say that it wasn't true, and that I never intentionally tried to attack or undermine anyone's authority, but it was useless. I left his office in tears. The pastor didn't know my wife was sitting just outside the door, which was open, or that she had heard the entire conversation. She, also, was in tears when I appeared in the doorway.

The man never spoke to me again, except in passing three days later—he ask how I was and then walked on. Although I'm sure no one else in the congregation realized it was me to whom the senior pastor and his associates were referring in many of the messages preached in the following weeks, it was still very painful to be preached against. I was referred to as the devil, compared to King Saul in the Old Testament, used as an example of losing the anointing of God, and called "Ichabod" (the glory of the Lord has departed, 1 Samuel 4:21)—all from the pulpit. After waiting three months for some kind of reconciliation to occur, and ignored as though I had never existed, I quietly left the church in October 1997. It was time to search for a new church to call home.

Since this senior pastor was a very influential man in our state, I knew my career as an ordained minister in our denomination was officially over. No pastor in Arizona would ever let me come and preach in his church now. It was hard enough to get pastors to cooperate before all this happened, let alone now that my character had been assassinated. So, I knew I was going to have to look at other denominations and start all over again to get credentials.

After much prayer, I decided to try not to burn any bridges with the people of our denomination, in case one day the Lord made it possible for me to return. I submitted a request to be medically retired and attached a doctor's letter providing medical evidence I was permanently and totally disabled. My request was approved and I was able to keep my credentials that I had worked so hard for.

Needless to say, these days were very difficult for MaryAnn and myself. I struggled with guilt and condemnation, believing maybe I really *was* a devil in saint's clothing—that God hated me and had thrown me away, among other terrible feelings. Thoughts of suicide flooded my mind continually. I even contemplated specific plans by which to end it all.

Had it not been for the grace of God and my love for my wife and children, I'm sure I would not be alive today. Because I didn't want to hurt my wife and kids and cause them any more pain by ending my life, I decided on several occasions not to go through with suicide plans. I felt like an empty shell—inside, I had already died and my relationship with God had become a war zone. The next four years of my life seemed like hell on earth. On the outside,

I tried to appear as though everything was fine, but on the inside, I was spiritually dead. Anything within me that represented life was being tortured with no apparent hope of deliverance. Of course, I couldn't keep much from my wife—MaryAnn was keenly aware of what was going on. She was determined to keep me alive and eventually resurrect my spiritual man. All kinds of spiritual challenges within our family took place as the kids tried to come to grips with the war going on inside of me.

In November of 1997, MaryAnn and I visited a nondenominational church in Tucson. A small light came on in the depths of my despair when we met Pastor Rick, who God eventually used to save my life. Pastor Rick loved MaryAnn and me back to spiritual health—a project which took four long years to accomplish.

The first time we visited his church, Pastor Rick spoke with us after the service and told us the Lord had told him I was a "pastor in crisis." Pastor Rick made an appointment with us to see him the next day. At the last moment we overcame reluctance and decided to go ahead with it. The office staff greeted us in a very cheerful way when we arrived. We told them we almost didn't come, and they responded that they had been praying all morning that we would keep the appointment.

I cried for over an hour in Pastor Rick's office as MaryAnn and I shared with him our story of what happened at the other church. He told us we were welcome to stay at his church for as long as we needed in order to be restored to spiritual health. He promised us unconditional love and that he would never do anything like what the previous pastor had done to us.

At Pastor Rick's church, the Lord opened the doors of ministry to us. Over that four-year period, we organized a team of forty people to go into the Apache reservation on a four-day, three-night evangelistic crusade. Another team went into Mexico, as well. We filled in as Youth Pastors for about two years and took the Missions Director position. Finally, we actually were achieving everything God told us we would do in that prophecy in my mother's church, back in Ohio in July of 1996!

The Lord slowly began to put the pieces back together for us. MaryAnn and I now recognize the mistakes we made leading up to those extremely difficult years. We know the pastor who fired me was merely an instrument the Lord used to teach us some very important lessons. Other reasons why we went through these trials, we may never understand until the day we meet our Maker. One thing we do know:

All things work together for good to those who love God, to those who are the called according to His purpose (Rom. 8:28).

Epilogue

Like most people, throughout my life I have had to go through many difficult times, especially after becoming a Christian. The struggles I faced in Turkey were only the beginning of years of suffering, poverty, and grief. Over the years, I have discovered the blessing behind every hardship. That blessing is a greater reliance on Jesus Christ, a deeper, fuller dependence on my Lord to carry me through, instead of relying on my own resources. I can truly say, "Greater is He that is in me, than he that is in the world" (1 John 4:4).

It is God's purpose to make us like Jesus. Jesus is our model, our forerunner—we are to follow Him, mimic Him, and be transformed into His image.

For whom He foreknew, He also predestined to be conformed to the image of His Son, that He might be the firstborn among many brethren (Rom. 8:29).

"But indeed, O man, who are you to reply against God? Will the thing formed say to him who formed it, 'why have you made me like this?'" (Rom. 9:20). Of course not. Nor can we question God concerning how or by what method He should use to make us like Jesus. Jesus said, "Most assuredly, I say to you, a servant is not greater than his master; nor is he who is sent greater than he who sent him" (John 13:16).

> *If the world hates you, you know that it hated Me before it hated you. If you were of the world, the world would love its own. Yet, because you are not of the world, but I chose you out of the world, therefore the world hates you. Remember the word that I said to you, "A servant is not greater than his master." If they persecuted Me, they will also persecute you. If they kept My word, they will keep yours also. But all these things they will do to you for My name's sake, because they do not know Him who sent Me* (John. 15:18–21).

We are not greater than Jesus Christ—if He suffered, we, too, must expect to suffer.

When it comes to suffering, we do have a choice—not whether or not we will accept the trial, but whether or not we will rejoice in the trial and draw closer to our God. We can decide to respond negatively and rebel against God. However, it is much easier to rejoice and draw closer to God than it is to throw a spiritual temper tantrum and rebel. Learn to look beyond pain and see God's purpose: a closer walk with your Lord, a stronger relationship, a greater commitment, spiritual maturity and a transformation into the same image of Jesus Christ. Yes, it is true:

> *All things work together for good to those who love God, to those who are the called* ACCORDING TO HIS PURPOSE (Rom. 8:28).

About the Author

Reverend Terry C. Barber was born on April 26, 1957, and raised in the north-central Ohio town of Ontario, just outside Mansfield. He attended Mount Union College in Canton, Ohio from 1975–1977, following his graduation from Ontario Senior High School in 1975.

He enlisted in the United States Air Force in May 1977, and was honorably discharged into the Air National Guard in October, 1978. Reverend Barber graduated in 1981 from East Texas Bible College, in Tyler, Texas. In 1982, he married his wife, MaryAnn Fetherston, and re-enlisted in the Air Force. Reverend Barber enrolled in correspondence courses at Berean University, Illinois, and was licensed to preach the gospel in 1990.

During the Gulf War, he served in the Air Force and was medically retired from the military in July, 1991. Reverend Barber was ordained as a Minister of the Gospel in 1992, after which he served as associate pastor and then senior pastor of various churches in upstate New York from 1989 to 1996. He also served in various capacities as an associate pastor in Arizona from 1997 to 2000, and is currently fully retired.